THE CHURCH AT THE
TURNING POINTS OF HISTORY

*To the Bishops, Priests, and Laymen who
have the courage and tenacity to remain at their stations
on the Barque of Peter as She faces into the most tempestuous
storm of her mighty history. May they remain unflinchingly
loyal to the Truth, serene at heart but vigorous in action,
and committed to steering Holy Mother Church
into calmer, more fruitful waters.*

# The Church at the Turning Points of History

## Godfrey Kurth
KNIGHT OF THE ORDER OF PIUS IX
DIRECTOR, BELGIAN HISTORICAL INSTITUTE AT ROME

INTRODUCTION BY PATRICK FOLEY, PH.D.

"I came, I saw, God conquered." —KING JOHN III, 1683

Norfolk, VA
2007

The Church at the Turning Points of History.
Copyright © 2007 IHS Press.
Preface, footnotes, typesetting, layout, and cover design
copyright 2007 IHS Press.
All rights reserved.

The present edition of *The Church at the Turning Points of History* is based upon the English translation made by Monsignor Victor Day, Vicar General of Helena, and published in 1918 by Naegele Printing Co., Helena, Montana. The translation was made from the fifth French edition of the work, *L'Eglise aux tournants de l'histoire*, published in Brussels in 1913 by Librairie Albert Dewit. The substance of the work is based upon a series of lectures given by the author to a Women's University Extension in Antwerp, 1897–1899. The original author's preface, which has been omitted in the present edition, explained that footnote citations were not provided for the facts cited, as most were presumed to be well known to readers, and the author begged that they "take his word" for the occasional facts that might be unfamiliar. Footnotes in the present edition are those added by Msgr. Day, with some modification by the editors. The spelling, punctuation, and formatting of the original edition have been largely preserved. Minor editorial corrections have been made to the text, and the original foreword to the 1918 English edition has been slightly abriged.

ISBN-13: 978-1-932528-11-4

ISBN: 1-932528-11-3

FRONTISPIECE: *Triumph of the Church*, a painting after Peter Paul Rubens (1577–1640), oil on wood, created sometime after 1628. In the image, the Church – symbolized by the Eucharist led by the Keys of Peter – has in bondage Blindness and Ignorance, and tramples Hatred, Discord, and Evil.

Library of Congress Cataloging-in-Publication Data

Kurth, Godefroid, 1847-1916.
 The church at the turning points of history / Godfrey Kurth ; introduction by Patrick Foley.
   p. cm.
 Originally published: Helena, Mont. : Naegele Printing Co., 1918.
 ISBN-13: 978-1-932528-09-1
 1. Church history. I. Title.
 BR145.3.K87 2007
 282.09--dc22

2007038611

Printed in the United States of America.

Gates of Vienna Books is an imprint of IHS Press, the only publisher dedicated exclusively to the social teachings of the Catholic Church.

For more information, contact:

IHS Press
222 W. 21st St., Suite F-122
Norfolk, VA 23517
info@ihspress.com • www.ihspress.com • 877-IHS-PRESS

# TABLE OF CONTENTS

INTRODUCTION . . . . . . . . . . . . . . . . . . . . . . . . 7
*by Patrick Foley, Ph.D.*

FOREWORD . . . . . . . . . . . . . . . . . . . . . . . . . . 17
*by Bishop John P. Carroll*

The Church at the Turning Points of History

    I. The Mission of the Church . . . . . . . . . . . . . . . . 21

    II. The Church and the Jews . . . . . . . . . . . . . . . . 27

    III. The Church and the Barbarians . . . . . . . . . . . . 37

    IV. The Church and Feudalism . . . . . . . . . . . . . . 45

    V. The Church and Neo-Caesarism . . . . . . . . . . . . 60

    VI. The Church and the Renaissance . . . . . . . . . . . 79

    VII. The Church and the Revolution . . . . . . . . . . . 97

NOTES . . . . . . . . . . . . . . . . . . . . . . . . . . . . . . 115

"In the history of mankind considered as a whole there are two grand divisions. On the one hand, there is the ancient world seated in the darkness of death; on the other hand, the modern world which advances in the light of the Gospel. This is, beyond compare, the greatest fact of history."

# INTRODUCTION

**O**N JANUARY 4, 1916, NOTED HISTORIAN GODFREY Kurth, C.S.G., died at Assche, Brabant. Professor Kurth, born at Arlon, Belgium, on May 11, 1847, with a lifelong dedication to the study of universal history, especially Europe's Catholic heritage, was regarded as one of the leading scholars of his day. At the time of his death he was serving in his tenth year as director of the Belgian Historical Institute at Rome. Prior to holding that position, Kurth had spent more than three and a half decades on the faculty of the State University of Liège, Belgium. Among the distinguished Catholic honors he had received or offices he held were: Knight of the Order of Pius IX; member of The Academy of the Catholic Religion (Rome); recipient of the doctorate *honoris causa* from the Catholic University of Louvain; and Commander of the Order of Leopold.

In addition Kurth was several times honored by being named a member of societies, academies, or institutes in London, Cologne, Leyden, Madrid, Barcelona, Rheims, and Belgium. He published numerous works on saints and historical personages such as Saints Clotilde and Boniface, Charles Martel, Charlemagne, the Merovingians, and King Philip II of Spain. Beyond these, he had other works published on various aspects of the histories of Belgium, Burgundy, the Frankish kingdoms, and other periods and regions of the European narrative. Most substantial as an overall work of Catholic history is his *Les Origines de la Civilisation Moderne* (*The Origins of Modern Civilization*), which ran to several editions during his lifetime. Without question, his *The Church at the Turning Points of History* (initially published in French as *L'Eglise aux Tournants de l'Histoire*) exists as his most accessible and, in some ways, most engaging tome. The book came into being as a published compilation of several major lectures he had presented over time on the broad topic of the mission of the Church as mirroring "the modern world which advances in the light of the Gospel . . . ."

## THE CHURCH AT THE TURNING POINTS OF HISTORY

When Kurth's book appeared on the scene in the early twentieth century, the Catholic world of scholarship was basking in the light of a revival of significant proportions that had developed earlier in the previous century, in England under the banners of John Henry Cardinal Newman and historian John Emerich Edward Dalberg-Acton, Lord Acton, and in the United States with the "use-primary-sources" approach to historical research and writing of John Gilmary Shea. This era of Catholic thinking, additionally, was later to see coming to the forefront, in the decades that followed, the influential writings of such giants as Hilaire Belloc, G.K. Chesterton, Evelyn Waugh, Christopher Dawson, and Jacques Maritain. Kurth's work, including *Turning Points,* made its own important contribution, between these two "eras," to this positive momentum.

Kurth studied the Church and her maturation, and considered them foundational to the substance of society at various turning points in history. He identified seven different points in the historical narrative of Western civilization wherein Catholicism's presence was of a particularly significant influence, and therefore in need of a clear portrayal. These Kurth analyzed with considerable accuracy. Such were the Mission of the Church; the Church and the Jews; the Church and the Barbarians; the Church and Feudalism; the Church and Neo-Caesarism; the Church and the Renaissance; and the Church and the Revolution. Each of these areas was to be investigated with the hope of developing major themes, ones which even today will be of great use in coming to understand more deeply, and thus better appreciate, the Catholic historical legacy to mankind.

An obvious strength of Kurth's book is the author's ability to seek historical truth and present it in a manner that would today be impossible, because of the modern atmosphere in which, quite often, veracity and frankness are left to suffer at the expense of various partisan agendas operative in the environment of "political correctness." Part and parcel of Kurth's effort to arrive at historical truth was his development of a number of subdivisions among his major areas of study. This allowed him to focus on specific personages, issues, movements, and so forth, in precise and objective terms.

In his first turning point of history, "The Mission of the Church," Professor Kurth focuses on the Church's understanding of her own

INTRODUCTION

purpose, and the way in which that understanding underlies her action through history. Moving from this broad subject, Kurth then addresses several considerations related to the history of "The Church and the Jews." These subdivisions analyze the ancient heritage of Christianity and its interaction with post-Incarnation Judaism, including a discussion of the significance of the Council of Jerusalem in A.D. 49. At the end of this section Kurth proclaims that this turning point of history showed the early Church at a period when Christianity was maturing as separate from rabbinical Judaism.

In analyzing his third turning point of history, "The Church and the Barbarians," Kurth argues that, "After three hundred years of a war of extermination, the Roman Empire had to acknowledge itself conquered by its victim...." Kurth here was referring to the Edict of Milan of A.D. 313, following the Emperor Constantine's victory at the Battle of Milvian Bridge the previous year, in which Constantine attributed his success to the Christian God. By the Edict of Milan, all Christians in the Roman Empire "who choose that religion [were] to be permitted to continue therein...." It was then that Christianity became legal throughout the Empire, and Kurth develops the historical reality that within a relatively short time Christianity in fact became the religion of the Empire and became linked with Roman civilization.

When dealing with the interaction between the Romans and the threatening Barbarians, Professor Kurth compares the Romans' fear of invasion during the fourth and early fifth centuries – which actually culminated in A.D. 410 with the Barbarian burning of Rome – to the concern that many had during his own time, in the early twentieth century, with the possibility of a future Asiatic incursion into Europe. Given the demographics of Europe today, Kurth's comparison has in ways proven to be insightful. Not only did Roman Christians, as well as others, see the sacking of Rome as the end of civilization, but the action of the Barbarians in fact drew the Church closer to the Roman civilization, a direction of movement identified with, Kurth points out, "the greatest Doctor of the Latin Church, St. Augustine." Here Kurth is referring to St. Augustine's profound work, *The City of God*. From that point of history onward, St. Augustine's *City of God* formed the major ideological base for a deeply developed Christian spiritual sense, not only of theological views, but of historical ones as well. Even today many historians are considered to be of the Augustinian school.

Following his reflections on the Church and the Barbarians, Professor Kurth searches laboriously into the historical turning point illustrated by the Church's action during the feudal period. As Kurth writes, the Church went from St. Boniface to Charlemagne to Alfred the Great, "and from the very first set herself to the task of bringing forth a new world." Making some pertinent observations about these three historical figures whose lives spanned 180 years, from A.D. 719 to 899, Professor Kurth then focuses his discussion of the Church and feudalism on secular attempts to interfere with the Church – especially the well-known issue of lay investiture. Directing the reader's attention to the Church's mission – which he refers to in these terms: "the Catholic Church is made for eternal rewards" – Kurth concludes that at that period in history the Church began to concentrate inwards, upon her "heart," drawing "a greater intensity and energy." Essential to that renewed perspective was the growing commitment to clerical reform, which in specific terms resulted in the Benedictine Cluniac Reforms, the evangelistic initiatives of Popes Leo IX and Gregory VII (Hildebrand), and the regularization of the election of pontiffs.

Following his candid discussion of the Church and Feudalism, Professor Kurth then turns his attention to what he calls "The Church and Neo-Caesarism." Kurth makes a strong argument, following the conclusion of his previous chapter, that as the Church had emerged victorious in the investiture struggle, she was from then onward, if only for a short time, able to emphasize her posture as the "supreme arbiter of the moral and religious life of the peoples . . . ." In that context, Kurth asserts that the Church had developed two aims: to pacify Europe, and in a united way to work against the advances of Islam. In covering these aspects of this period, Kurth highlights the accomplishments of the A. D. 1122 Concordat of Worms, wherein the State recognized "freedom of [the Church's] canonical elections" and her complete sovereignty in her own domain.

This chapter is, in my estimation, one of his most intriguing. Kurth centers his attention here, among other things, on the papacy's hopes for a truce between nations. Relating to that aim was the hope of the papacy

# INTRODUCTION

that Europe would form a front against "the Crescent" – Kurth's frank way of identifying Islam after the Turks' conquest of Constantinople in 1453 established the crescent as the symbol of Islam. In one remark of great interest, Kurth writes that he sees in this ideal of the leaders of the Church attempting to lead Europe in defense of itself a forerunner of sorts of later prominent Catholic personages such as, among others, St. Joan of Arc and Christopher Columbus. He also courageously adds, "And we may hope that it will also be the ideal of Europe, when a re-christianized Europe will have become reconciled with the ideal."

Pursuing these issues further, Kurth goes on in this chapter to write about emerging national and state challenges to the papacy, and related challenges coming from the lay society – a society built upon laicism and an exaggerated state nationalism. Professor Kurth makes an incisive point, one often ignored in modern historiography, that the Catholic spirit of the Middle Ages had for a time and on several occasions in fact triumphed over the theories of Neo-Caesarism. In making such a statement, Kurth was referring to the historical reality that on the ruins of the empire, the demolition of which the emperors themselves, through their ambition, had caused, the Catholic spirit had "kept intact the great principle of the Christian republic of the Middle Ages."

Demonstrating the historical depth of his insights, Professor Kurth then provides us with a profoundly accurate assessment of the destructive nature of French King Philip IV's declarations attempting to deny the Pope a role as mediator *based upon his ecclesiastical authority,* even while accepting that the Pope could in practical terms act as such a mediator between warring nations. The Pope, Philip IV argued, could become involved only as a private person and as a "chosen mediator." In essence, Philip IV was proclaiming the separation of church and state, and, as Kurth suggests, the monarch's views were to be baneful for the future society of Europe. Politics, according to Philip IV, *were to be divorced from morality,* especially morality as defined by Christian law. This vision contradicted a Christian historical tradition that had existed since the days of the early Christians, and as made formal by the theory of Pope St. Gelasius I, who reigned from March 1, 492, to November 21, 496. Thus Professor Kurth perceives, correctly, in my view, that separation of church and state – so well known to modern

American society as a misrepresentation of the First Amendment of the Constitution – actually meant removing politics from the environs of morality based upon natural law.

Kurth's analysis of this issue is profound, both intellectually and spiritually. Discussing the character and impact of Pope Boniface VIII's bull *Unam Sanctam* of November 8, 1302, wherein it is asserted that it is necessary for every person, for his salvation, to be subject to the Roman Pontiff, Kurth makes clear the historical veracity of Pope Boniface VIII's actions. Perhaps most useful in guiding us to a truthful interpretation of history is his placing of this whole episode within the historical and societal boundaries known to the Europe of the time, rather than offering simply a condemnation of Boniface VIII as a reactionary, as many historians do today. In fact, Kurth even notes how French historians of his day had exonerated Boniface VIII as having acted in the same manner as would have previous popes. Finally, in this chapter Kurth draws the obvious conclusion that as the Christian republic itself was destroyed, nations were torn away from the guidance of the Church, and they have yet to make their way back.

At the very beginning of his chapter discussing "The Church and the Renaissance," Professor Kurth identified the major misconception governing the standard approach to this period in history. He asserts that, "What really took place [in the Renaissance] was not so much a revival of learning as a flowering out of the learning of the previous centuries." Relying on the teaching of St. Thomas Aquinas that from nothing comes nothing, Kurth argued that the Renaissance grew – and must have grown – from the Middle Ages. Indeed, the view that the Renaissance was a further development of earlier learning is built upon an acceptance of what the previous era had accomplished, and what was already embedded in the Christian society of the time preceding the Renaissance: the founding of schools, colleges, and universities; the formulation of disciplines of study (the seven pillars of wisdom); study of languages, literature, theology, history, and more. But Kurth also stresses, of course, that an unbridled admiration for antiquity during the fifteenth and sixteenth centuries led to an exaggeration of the literary merits of the pagan world, which in turn could and did lead some people at various times to a contempt for Christianity.

# INTRODUCTION

From "The Church and the Renaissance," Professor Kurth moves on to discuss his final turning point in history: the interaction between the Church and the Revolution. Initially focusing on the bloody substance of the Revolution, Kurth quickly turns his attention to the Revolution's attack on the *ancien régime*. As a distinct aspect of that coverage, Kurth's treatment of French society at the time of the outbreak of the Revolution in 1789 differs from that of many other historians. He maintains that the coming of the Revolution and its atrocities could never be regarded as having *alone* been caused by abuses of the *ancien régime*. Kurth insists that French society in 1789 was still quite religious, polite, and satisfied with the reign of Louis XVI, and he notes several positive accomplishments of Louis XVI, steps that the king took to help his subjects. In fact, what Professor Kurth saw as the main cause of the Revolution was the emerging dominance of the pre-revolutionary intellectual world by antireligious "free thinkers." As these came to the fore, they pushed the revolutionary movement beyond its initial stages and channeled it toward the destruction of the *ancien régime* and especially the Catholic Church. Recently, a highly respected French historian, Guillaume Bertier de Sauvigny, made a statement that confirms Professor Kurth's view: "In religious matters the *philosophes* [i.e., the free thinkers] violently attacked the Catholic Church for her [alleged] ignorance and intolerance."

In this context Kurth stresses the influence of Voltaire, under a subheading entitled "Unbelief and licentiousness fostered by Voltaire." Indeed, Professor Kurth refers to Voltaire as "the most complete incarnation of the irreligious spirit of the eighteenth century." Kurth also makes a strong point that Voltaire was surrounded by defenders of impiety, atheists who hated Christianity and even criticized Voltaire for believing in God. It was that group of licentious thinkers, greatly under the influence of the *Encyclopédie*, who claimed to give to society "a summary of all knowledge" but instead brought disaffection with Christianity, especially Catholicism, to much of the French population. It was in that environment that, as Kurth indicates, the radical character of the French Revolution developed, ultimately causing the breach between it and the Church.

There are places in the book where any number of historians and other scholars, Catholic and non-Catholic, might disagree with Kurth's perspectives on the history touched upon in *Turning Points*. One area that one might credibly wonder about is both the content and the rather "prophetic" nature of his final subsection, entitled "New awakening of Christian society." There can be no doubt that, at the time of its writing, the atmosphere for a Catholic intellectual moment, as well as for a serious penetration of social and political life by Catholicism, was ripe. But what a turn things took between the time when Kurth's last lecture, forming the final chapter of this book, was delivered in 1898, and now, when Christian society, by all human reckoning, is in retreat, godless globalism marches forward unabated, wars and rumors of wars abound, and the authority conceded to the Church by modern man is anything but the assessment that Professor Kurth offered in claiming that no one would then deny that "the Catholic Church is the highest authority"! What Kurth perhaps did not see, like so many others, was the continuing advance of secular liberalism, with its corrosive ability to destroy the willingness, if not the capacity, of even the non-Catholic, secular mind to recognize the truth of the natural law, and the historical and philosophical validity of Catholicism's claims.

No doubt when Kurth writes, as a Catholic, that "the triumph of the Catholic cause is secure," he is speaking a *supernatural* truth. But from a human point of view, such a triumph is never secure, and we make bold to say that he would have admitted – indeed, he *did* implicitly admit – such a thing, having made note in fact of "the Catholic spirit [that] has taken possession of public life." For it was indeed that seizure of initiative by the Catholic clergy and laity, and the assertion of Catholic thought in sociology, art, science, and indeed "in all manifestations of the intellectual and moral life of the people" that gave Kurth his hope and confidence in predicting ultimate triumph; and it is the considerable absence of those things today that forces us to note the inaccuracy of his prophesy. Indeed what becomes clear from the divergence between Kurth's prediction and our present reality is just how dependent upon human action God allows our human predicament to be. For the triumph of the Church may be assured, in spirit, at the end of time, but her triumph in the here and now, with all the philosophical and social realities that accompany such a triumph on the temporal plane, depend upon the "Catholic battalions [being] reorganized; [and]

# INTRODUCTION

on every side an army of laymen...rising." If the triumph of the Catholic cause is not today assured as Kurth then felt it to be, it is not because the Church's claims and essence are any less real, but because, in his words, "the recruits" have insufficiently "rallied about their banner." An answer as to whether they will do so sufficiently in the future is better left to the prophet than to the historian – because it is the past which is the latter's purview, and not the future. As Fordham historian and Professor Ross J. S. Hoffman wrote not so long ago, "it is more proper for us to pray than to prophesy."

Nevertheless, and in spite of this ultimate observation, it cannot be questioned that Professor Kurth offers us his deep understanding of history, especially that of Christendom and later Europe. And along with that he offers his keen perception of the substantive presence of the Catholic Church, at virtually all historical periods and social levels, in bringing European civilization to its fullness, as well as even the cultures of other regions of the world that Catholic Europe deeply touched. Godfrey Kurth's work should be studied by every person genuinely interested in a truthful picture of the Catholic Church at the turning points of history.

        Patrick Foley, Ph.D.
        September 15, 2007
        The Seven Sorrows of the Blessed Virgin Mary

"Human society is drawn instinctively in the direction of Jesus Christ whenever it obeys the laws of self-preservation. The spirit of evil may do its worst, it will but precipitate events and hasten the day when humanity will have choice only between Catholic civilization and revolutionary anarchy....

"We would indeed be blind to the teachings of history were we, at this stage of her life, to forget that now, as in the past, the Church is upholding not the interests of a class but the cause of humanity."

# FOREWORD

THE MISSION OF THE CHURCH IS TO ALL NATIONS AND to all ages. The doctrines of the Church must be always and everywhere the same, namely those her Divine Founder commanded her to preach. To teach them effectively, however, she must sympathize with the manners, customs and institutions of the various peoples she meets across the centuries, adapting herself to their genius, to their forms of civilization. Like the Apostle, she must "become all things to all men, that she may save all." Hence, she has been obliged in the course of her history to break with old systems and organizations with which her life had become interwoven, in order to conform to new conditions of human society. This was not an easy thing to do. It always entailed a struggle. It often meant a crisis in her work of evangelization. If she were a mere human institution, she could not, anymore than the other human institutions whose wrecks strew the highway of history, have survived the onslaughts that have been made upon her. That she has passed every crisis and triumphantly outridden every storm that has beaten upon her for nearly two thousand years is evidence of the divinity of her mission to the nations and to the ages.

Her first struggle was with the judaizing influences which surrounded her cradle. Jewish thought and sentiment and practices threatened to restrict her work to the Jews and to those who would be willing to accept Jewish religious traditions and customs. In the Council of Jerusalem she took the bold step that enabled her to break away from her Jewish moorings and take to the high seas of the Gentile world – to encounter storms and tempests, but also to enclose in her net the copious draught of fishes. From that time forward she emphasized the universal character of her mission, and, in the language of the Apostle, became a debtor to Gentile and Jew alike.

Again, when she had converted the Gentile world and ruled humanity from the very capital of civilization, there was danger that her destinies had become irrevocably linked with those of the Roman Empire. Hence, when the Barbarian invasions had sounded the knell of Roman civilization, many thought the Church would disappear in the great cataclysm. But true to her universal mission, she offered the message of salvation to the Barbarians. These accepted the cross and carried it, together with the Christian civilization of which it is the symbol, to the remotest corners of the old Roman world.

The converted Barbarians in the gratitude of their hearts lavished upon the Church the wealth they had amassed, and Barbarian kings shared with her bishops and priests their own temporal rulership over the people. The prestige and power thus given to the Church became in time a real menace to her. In exchange for it kings persuaded themselves that they had a right to select candidates for vacant sees and abbacies. The kings of Germany even went so far as to arrogate to themselves the nomination of the Sovereign Pontiff, and for a period of about one hundred years no Pope could ascend the chair of Peter without their approbation or consent. Under such a system royal favor and willingness to do the bidding of the king, rather than priestly virtue, became the chief qualifications for ecclesiastical dignities. The result was that simony and a general laxity of morals grew apace among the clergy, and heresy began to make inroads upon the people. The Church was stripped of her independence in things spiritual and became a mere creature of the State. Feudalism had, indeed, enriched her, but it was at the price of chains and slavery.

The evil was grave beyond all precedent. And yet, with the vitality guaranteed to the Church by divine promise, her great heart slowly drove out from her almost atrophied body the fatal infection and clothed it again with health and liberty. The fire of Christian and priestly life which had not wholly died out, was fanned into a flame; Pope Leo IX and his two successors, by taking possession of the Pontifical See only after the prescriptions of the canon law had been complied with, prepared the way for the constitution of Nicholas II on the election of Sovereign Pontiffs; and the open warfare of Gregory VII, the immortal Hildebrand, on the right of Lay Investiture triumphed in the Concordat of Worms, the State giving back to the Church complete freedom in all canonical elections.

This was the greatest triumph of the Church. Free from the embrace of Feudalism, she extinguished heresy, united Europe in defence of the

Holy Sepulchre, brought Gothic art to its highest perfection, created the great universities, placed saints upon the thrones of kings, became the supreme authority of the West and the spiritual oracle of the world.

Independent in her own spiritual domain, the Church had succeeded in uniting all the states of Europe in one grand Christian republic, of which the Pope was the acknowledged spiritual chieftain. In the quarrels of kings with one another or with their subjects, the Pope was the supreme arbitrator. His decisions were final, because they had back of them the moral sanction which the common acceptance of Christian principles made effective. This happy condition was not to last. The spirit of nationalism, jealous of whatever savored of foreign interference, fostered by a laicizing movement envious of the social prestige of the clergy and directed by a general infatuation for Roman law, gradually developed a condition favorable to royal absolutism. The death of Pope Boniface VIII and the triumph of Philip the Fair widened the breach between the Church and the State, and hastened the day when kings everywhere would proclaim political maxims to be independent of religious belief and absolve themselves from conformity to the principles of Christian morality in the conduct of their realms – hastened the day when national policy would be no longer regulated by the moral standard which Christianity had set up for the individual – the day when monarchs, disregarding the ecumenical character of the Church of Christ, would establish state religions of their own making. It was the old autocracy of the Roman Caesars, who arrogated to themselves the title of king and pontiff, brought back again to earth – an autocracy which Christianity had banished from the world. The Church could only protest and, sitting at the foot of the cross, await the return of better days.

Since kings refused the moral guidance of the Church and became a law unto themselves, it was only natural that the influence of the Church in securing obedience to the royal authority was weakened. The bad example of the kings had its effect upon their subjects. The Church had, indeed, captured the Renaissance and made it issue in that grand efflorescence of Christian art and architecture, of poetry and music, of painting and sculpture, which will never cease to command the admiration of the world. But the by-products of the Renaissance were free thought and licentiousness.

# THE CHURCH AT THE TURNING POINTS OF HISTORY

That the French Revolution swept away the altar as well as the throne is not surprising when we consider that the intellectual and moral distemper referred to above had for a long time been working in the bosom of the nation. For nearly five hundred years the Church had been excluded from the political councils of the country and deprived of the vitalizing power that comes from the fearless profession of the doctrine of the supreme headship of the Sovereign Pontiff. The clergy belonged to a privileged order and were held responsible before the bar of public opinion for the mistakes of the regime of which they were supposed to form a part. Prelates and priests, notwithstanding the irreproachable private lives of the vast majority, lacked intellectual courage and accepted the humiliation of the Church. In a word, the Church was not properly represented in France during the times which begot the Revolution. If she had been, in the full vigor of her apostolate, either the monarchy would have been shorn of its autocratic power, or the forces of the Revolution would have been directed along the lines of Christian teachings.

But the failure of the Church was local and temporary. If she slept during the days of the French Revolution, it was like the sleep of Jesus in the tempest-tossed bark of Peter. To some her awakening may seem tardy, but it is an awakening as fruitful as was that of the Master. Her great Pontiff, Leo XIII, in immortal encyclicals, which have become the textbook of statesmen the world over, has proclaimed the Christian constitution of states and the Magna Carta of the laboring man's liberties. And Benedict XV is heard above the roar of battle urging the warring nations to respect the old principles of Christian morality as the only means of mitigating the horrors of war and of securing a just and lasting peace.

Such are the considerations which Godfrey Kurth puts before us in his book, entitled *The Church at the Turning Points of History*. To those who desire a comprehensive view of the great crises in the history of Christian civilization we cheerfully recommend this really great work.

John P. Carroll<br>
Bishop of Helena<br>
February 22, 1918

THE CHURCH AT THE
TURNING POINTS OF HISTORY

Chapter I

THE MISSION OF THE CHURCH

IN THE HISTORY OF MANKIND CONSIDERED AS A WHOLE there are two grand divisions. On the one hand, there is the ancient world seated in the darkness of death; on the other hand, the modern world which advances in the light of the Gospel. This is, beyond compare, the greatest fact of history.

*Christianity opens new era for humanity.*

The opposition between these two worlds is sharp and well-defined. The line of demarcation which separates them is very clearly drawn. It is not an imperceptible and gradual evolution that leads humanity from the one to the other. It is rather a new spiritual influence, a mighty impulse which brings about an immediate and radical change. We know the precise date of this great change, and we have taken that date as the starting point of our chronology. It is the Christian era that opens the annals of a new creation and a new humanity.

What is the vital principle of this new creation? It is the new ideal brought into the world by Jesus Christ, or, to adhere to the simplicity of the Gospel language, it is what Jesus Christ Himself calls the New Law. Deposited within the bosom of humanity as leaven in the paste – this comparison is also His – it produces there the marvellous fermentation that transforms the most refractory elements. Allow this leaven to do its work. The more it acts the more substantial and nourishing will be the bread of civilization.

*Christianity offers supreme happiness to all.*

The principle of Christian civilization is essentially opposed to that of ancient society. Compare the two worlds: on the surface you perceive many characteristics common to both, but at the bottom of these common traits you perceive the irreducible contradiction of the fundamental idea on which they were based. There is question not merely of a difference of degree, but of a difference of nature, which has a bearing on a most important matter, on the most vital interests of humanity. The two societies differ in their respective conception of life and the solution they give to the problem of existence.

Antiquity has never proposed this problem in formal terms; moreover the ancients lacked both the courage and the knowledge required to solve it. In practice, however, they have always given the wrong solution. Christianity has proposed the question boldly and has answered it in a triumphant manner.

Why has man been placed in this world, and what is the end of his existence here below? Must he be only the ephemeral spectator of the tableau of creation, or the unconscious instrument of some mission higher than his own, or the lamentable plaything of blind forces that dispute the possession of his senses and of his heart? Is he, with the contradictions that are at the root of his being, and with his boundless aptitude for suffering, the abortive child of this world and the plaything of an eternal illusion? Has he a future to conquer, an end to attain, and are this future and this end worth the effort they cost him? Or is he only a fortuitous and lamentable combination of elements associated for the time in a community of joys and of sufferings, to be finally disassociated and recomposed later on in the eternal circle of pitiless fatalities?

Christianity answers these questions with absolute clearness and certitude.

Man is not a child of chance – he is the creature of God. God has made him the king of creation. He has given him a mind to know Him, a heart to love Him, and a will to be in accord with His own. He has opened before him the way he must follow, He has taught him the law he must observe, He has promised him eternal happiness as the reward for fidelity in serving Him. In other words, He has made the fidelity of man to the Supreme Being the condition of his supreme happiness.

*Paganism brings empty pleasures to few.*

This is the teaching of Christianity. In this promise all religions and philosophies join Christianity. But, unable to rise with her to the pure and high sources whence flows the true happiness of the human race, they flutter about with their short wings in a common and feverish aspiration for happiness. They also promise happiness to men, but they do not understand it as Christianity does. The good, in which they make men hope to find this happiness, has none of the qualities that give it stability. It is not absolute, it is not pure, it is not eternal. It is a sum of joys that do not go beyond the duration of time, the boundaries of earth, or the reach of mankind. In a word, it is not happiness, but pleasure; – sometimes pleasure of a higher order, when, as with elevated souls, it consists in the intoxication of glory; other times pleasure of a low and degrading kind, when, as with the multitude, it limits itself to the gross pleasures of the senses. In every case, whether it be intellectual or material, it is but the shadow, or to speak better, it is only the appearance of happiness. And yet this sort of pleasure – and this alone – antiquity had the courage to promise to men, and the power to procure for some of them. And antiquity never meant anything else when there was mention of *Roman felicity* – that fiction so dear to the statesmen of the Empire of the Caesars.

Quite a complicated machinery was needed to realize this paltry happiness. It was necessary to place in common the powers of all men, and to deposit them in the hands of a being produced by their collectivity – the State. Invested with all the power and the rights which before could have resided in all and in each of its members, the State undertook to procure for them the sum of all the enjoyments which constituted their ideal of happiness. These enjoyments may be summed up in two words: idleness and voluptuousness. To eat one's bread without labor and to pass one's time in amusement was, to use a familiar and at the same time a very exact phrase, the *maximum* of felicity as the ancient State understood it.

It was not much, and, nevertheless, how few could enjoy this meagre happiness. It could be the lot of but a small minority. If a man lives without work, he forces others to work for him; if he lives for pleasure, it is necessary for him to have an army of people who will furnish him amusement. There existed, therefore, legions of slaves of every kind to procure bread and pleasure for the favorites of the State; the terrestrial paradise of the chosen few had for its correlative the terrestrial hell of the multitude. Even at this price, were the elect sure of their happiness? No: they wasted away with disgust and weariness. For such is the inexorable providential law attached to the abuse of earthly pleasures. Pleasure, chosen as an end, is a cruel god who devours his adorers. In the midst of pleasure the happy ones of the world felt themselves taken at the throat by the lurking hand of death which crouched within their poisoned joys. They saw these sources of prosperity that formerly were fed by the sacred sweat of labor dry up around them. The Empire was no longer defended except by Barbarians; public works were carried on only by slaves; the fields, deserted by the farmer, were fruitless; the ranks of human society began to thin out in a dreadful manner. Happiness, as understood by the ancient world, was nothing but the slow suicide of society. Thus, universal misery sprang from the very principle of the civilization that had promised to its votaries happiness here below.

The happiness Christianity promises to man presents a sum of characteristics radically opposed to those of the *Roman felicity*. It consists in the enjoyment of a Supreme Being, that is to say, in the union with God. It is perfect like the Good which is its principle, it is indefectible, it is eternal, it is made for all on the sole condition that they obey the law of love: – to love God above all things and one's neighbor as oneself. The happiness of the pagan is not possible without the corresponding misery of the majority of the human race. The Christian cannot be truly happy unless he makes as many as possible of his fellow men participate in his happiness. He does this directly by the daily practice of charity, and indirectly by mortification and labor. By mortifying himself he frees those who minister to his pleasures; by working he produces a wealth that increases the well-being of others. In principle, a Christian society is a society of brothers, just as in principle, a pagan society is a society of slaves.

# THE MISSION OF THE CHURCH

*The Church is reservoir of divine life of Christianity.*
It is not enough to know the difference – or better, the opposition – between these two principles. It is necessary also to see how the Christian principle was able to implant itself in human society notwithstanding the violence which it does to human nature, how it could continue in existence notwithstanding the bitter war which all the passions have declared against it, how it has succeeded in becoming the guide and the light of the better part of the human race. Why does the word which has promulgated the New Law always dominate the development of our civilization, as an ideal acclaimed even by those who misunderstand it; while so many other golden words, fallen from the lips of the ancient sages, have suffered the lot of those delicious perfumes which are exhaled by some choice flower but which, after having for a time perfumed the neighborhood, scattered and vanished in the air without leaving a trace save in the memory?

Christian faith answers that this word is a divine word, and that the words of Jesus Christ, according to His promise, will not pass away. But the Christian, who seeks to give an account of his faith, is not forbidden to study the manner in which Providence assures to His word the indefectible authority it should have over men. If Christianity has been more than a sublime philosophical doctrine, if it has been a principle of life and of action which has permeated, quickened, and transformed the world, it is because, from the first, it was so constituted that it could live and perpetuate itself on earth. It was clothed with a living body which became the agent of its transcendent action; this body is the Church.

The Church, with her powerful and incorruptible organism, is the reservoir of the divine life of Christianity, distributing this life and renewing it at its source. She has been created perfect, because to fulfil her mission she must have in herself the principle of life; sovereign, that she may be fettered by no one; universal, to embrace all men; indefectible, to extend to all generations. It is in her and by her that the human race realizes its supernatural mission, which is the conquest and the enjoyment of the Supreme Good. She assumes the direction of the moral life, but leaves to the State a portion beautiful enough. This portion is the earth which the State has at all times claimed and striven to obtain. The Church reserves for herself heaven in which the State has no concern.

The State is the society of bodies, the Church, of souls. The former is the kingdom of men, the latter is the Kingdom of God. The Church does not declare war on the State, she extends to it the hand of friendship. If the State helps the Church, she blesses it; if the State respects her liberties, she asks nothing more; if the State attacks these liberties, she sheds her blood rather than allow it. For she cannot renounce her mission. She has received charge to teach all nations. She is responsible to God for the salvation of humanity and, with regard to this duty, every man has the right to call her to account.

*How the Church fulfils her mission.*

How has the Church fulfilled her mission? During the course of the nineteen centuries just elapsed, has she always grasped the many and changeable problems that have confronted her? Has she, like the father of the family spoken of in the Gospel, known how to draw from her treasure the eternal truths which admit of no compromise, together with the new applications which vary according to the diversity of time and place? Has she known how to speak their language to all the centuries she has traversed, and to familiarize herself with the genius of all the peoples she has met on her way? Has she been, has she truly remained, that universal and indefectible society that contains within itself all civilization, or would she be merely one of those fleeting forms, in which, at a given moment, the human race embodied its ever changing aspirations? This is the question which it behooves us to answer in the lectures that will follow.

It is a grand panorama that will be unrolled. I dare say, there is none grander in all history, nor is there any more instructive. It is not for me to deduce in advance its teachings; but from the very outset who could doubt of their bearing and eloquence? They will, I hope, speak loud enough to be understood without much mental effort. Our ambition will be more modest and at the same time more elevating than the wild fancy of the ancient Greek philosopher Pythagoras, who believed he heard the harmony produced by the eternal movement of the spheres. We will strive to understand the voice that issues forth from the great phenomena of history, and which is, in a certain measure, the voice of God.

Chapter II

# THE CHURCH AND THE JEWS

I N THIS LECTURE I SHALL TRY TO ANSWER THIS QUESTION: How did Christianity become a universal religion? At first sight it would seem that this is not a question at all. At this day it is indeed beyond question that Christianity is by its nature the religion of humanity and that once she had received her mission to preach the Gospel to every creature she could not shirk it without perishing. But these considerations, which are enough for the faith of the believer, do not satisfy the curiosity of the historian. For what interests the historian is not merely the terminal of the journey but the course of travel as well. The question under consideration comes then to this: What obstacles hindered Christianity from becoming a universal religion? *And how did she succeed in overcoming them?*

*Christianity hindered in expansion by question of Ancient Law.*

The great obstacles, or, rather, the chief danger that the Church encountered in the first years lay in her ignorance of the attitude to be assumed concerning the Ancient Law and Israel. The lapse of time has solved this problem clearly and with precision, and now it is within the grasp of a child. There is nothing now in common between Israel rejected, shut up within her synagogue, and the people of God gathered about the Church. But it was quite different when the Church came into being. Far from considering Israel as the people of reprobation, the Christians, one and all – the Apostles at their head – continued to regard the Jews as the people of God. Being Jews themselves and holding fast to the Law of Moses, they saw in Christianity the complement of the Law and in the Church the consummate flower that came forth to crown the fertile root of Jesse.

### *Christian Church Jewish in origin.*

And how could they have believed otherwise? For centuries Israel had waited for the Messiah, who was to come according to the promise of the prophets to establish the kingdom of God, and to bring upon earth the reign of justice and peace. It mattered not whether this kingdom was of a temporal order – as the greater part of the Jews believed – or of the spiritual order – as the Christians admitted from the beginning – this much was certain to them all:- it was to be the kingdom of Israel. Was it not the people of Israel who had received the divine promises? Was it not Abraham to whom it had been foretold that his posterity would be as numerous as the stars of heaven, and was it not David to whom God had announced that he had made a covenant with his house and that from him should come forth the Desired of all Nations? Was not Israel the guardian of the Law, of that Law which Christ said He had come to fulfil and not to destroy? And had He not said further that He had come first for the wandering sheep of the flock of Israel, and had He not recommended His Apostles to preach the Gospel first to the Jews?

How, then, could the Church have been to men of that time other than an extension of Israel, a new budding forth of Jacob? She was wholly Jewish: her Divine Founder was a Jew, the apostles and disciples were Jews, the first converts also were Jews. The three thousand persons whom Saint Peter baptized at Jerusalem on the day of Pentecost were Jews *of the dispersion*; and he addressed Jews exclusively, when he said: "Therefore let all the house of Israel know most certainly that God hath made both Lord and Christ, this same Jesus, whom you have crucified." (Acts II, 36) And later, when the apostles and disciples carried the Gospel beyond Judea, they tarried only in the towns where there were Jews, stayed in the Jewish quarters, frequented the synagogues, and it was there they announced to all that the Messiah of the prophets had come and that He was called Jesus of Nazareth. In a word, everywhere, throughout the entire world as at Jerusalem, the Church was sinking its roots deep into the synagogue, and the first Christian congregations were in truth assemblies of Jews.

### *Gentile converts required to become naturalized Jews.*

This does not mean that this Christian Church of Jewish nationality wished to close her doors to the Gentiles. On the contrary, she dreamed of gathering within her embrace all the people of the earth, in order to comply with the demand of Christ. The Jewish people themselves never exercised towards the rest of humanity that absolute isolation which ill-informed historians impute to them. At all times they strove to win to their faith the children of other nations, and their proselytism was as active as it was sincere. The Gospel itself gives testimony of this in these words: "Woe to you scribes and Pharisees: because you go round about the sea and the land to make one proselyte: and when he is made, you make him the child of hell twofold more than yourselves."

Thus the people of Israel were surrounded by a throng of proselytes. One class of proselytes were called *Proselytes of the Gate*, because they were permitted to pass only the first gate of the court of the temple: they were such as acknowledged the true God, abstained from all idolatry and observed the seven precepts of the natural law. The second class were called *Proselytes of Righteousness*, and were those who accepted the whole Jewish religion and who pledged themselves to observe all the precepts without exception. Initiated through the rite of circumcision, they had the same rights and the same duties as the Israelites by birth.

In general, in order to become servers of the true God, the proselytes were obliged, if I may use a modern expression, to become naturalized Jews:- this was the absolute condition. The Proselytes of Righteousness possessed, in virtue of the rite of circumcision, their final naturalization papers; henceforth they became part not only of the synagogue, but of the Jewish nation. The Proselytes of the Gate, initiated in a manner less complete, saw themselves excluded, by that very fact, from participation in the Jewish worship; the temple remained closed to them; they were but the protégés and clients of Israel, or, if you like, they were Jews of second rank. In a word, without denying to anyone the right to adore with her the true God, Israel expected each worshiper to receive from her, in some way, the investiture, to become a Jew in more or less measure according to the right he wished to enjoy. The Jews regarded themselves as forming within the family of the servers of God the central nucleus, the circle of the elite; they meant to be to the rest of humanity what Levi had been within his fold, the race marked forever with a sign of predilection, the priestly tribe which stood as the intermediary between God and man.

Such was the Jewish viewpoint, which the first Christians, Jews themselves, carried with them into Christianity. They saw in the

Church a synagogue of superior order to which God had revealed the obscure meaning of the prophecies, but a synagogue nevertheless into which no one could enter without being a member either by birth or by adoption of the people of Israel. Now then, I ask, was this really the way to bring nations to embrace the Gospel – to oblige them to give up their nationality as well as their religion? When one sees even today the injury that national susceptibilities, often the best founded, cause to the Catholic apostolate and to the advance of the Gospel, it can be surmised what would have been the result if at that time, there had been imposed upon nations the most unbearable of all humiliations – national renouncement. Allow me to illustrate by an example. If today the German Lutherans, the English Episcopalians, the Russian Schismatics and other peoples whom we desire to unite within the unity of faith were told that in order to become Catholic they must first become Frenchmen, do you think it would hasten their conversion and that there would be any hope of seeing them make profession of our faith? And yet France is a great and glorious nation, enjoying the respect of all, even of those who hate her; while the Jews were a little nation universally despised, an object of hatred to the whole human race (as Tacitus states), about whom were spread most repugnant tales. For a Greek or a Roman to renounce his national title and become a Jew would have meant not only to give up his national traditions but also to embrace cheerfully opprobrium and ridicule, by assuming a nationality that was in a way under the ban of civilization.

### *Christian Church without light on subject.*

Here we see how Israel by her pretensions to leadership in the kingdom of God hindered the propagation of the Gospel. So long as Israel stood between the Savior and the human race, the human race was bound to keep away from the Savior. This is plain to us of modern times who look at this epoch at the distance necessary for clear vision and who have sufficient freedom of mind to form a fair judgment. But such was not the position of those who, whether Christian or Jew, lived in the midst of occurring events without being able to foresee their course. How could they foresee it without being prophets? And how would they have dared to choose a line of conduct without a special revelation? The apostles themselves were without light upon this weighty problem. The Gospels did not furnish them with the solution. They were children of Israel and they had to be on their guard lest they should lay themselves open to calumny; under the conditions, could they have been other – should they have been other – than good patriots and faithful observers of the Law of Moses? And this they were – all of them. The most finished type of the true Jew, whom all the Jews venerated and delighted to call the Just, was himself an apostle, nay more, he was a relative of Jesus – known as St. James the Less. Certainly, these are not the sort of men who could guess the danger that threatened the Church in its deadly grapple with Judaism, much less break the bond that seemed to tie the Church forever to the synagogue.

Thus, humanly speaking, Christianity found itself in its early days in a blind alley. It remained a national religion, it was not becoming a universal religion. It was merely a phenomenon of the inner history of Judaism, a religious revolution that could arouse only the Jews, and attract to itself only the scornful curiosity of the rest of the world. The pagan world would hear only the little that was said of it by the Roman historians, Suetonius and Tacitus, namely, that a little nation which on account of its fanaticism was consigned to the execration of humanity had one day been set in turmoil by innovations preached within its fold by a certain Chrestus and that in order to end these troubles the Jews had been expelled from Rome.

*Vision of Peter solves problem – Baptism of Cornelius.*

It was at this moment that there occurred the extraordinary scene of which the Acts account. I ask permission to reproduce this sacred page; none more fateful is found in the history of Christianity.

There was in the city of Caesarea, in Palestine, a centurion of the Roman army, named Cornelius. He was a just man and God-fearing. One day an angel appeared to him saying that his prayers had been agreeable to the Lord, and that he was to send for one Simon Peter who was then living at Joppe, in the house of a tanner by the seaside. Cornelius obeyed and despatched three men to the Apostle. I leave the words to the inspired text:

> And on the next day whilst they were going on their journey, and drawing nigh to the city, Peter went up to the higher parts of the house to pray about the sixth hour.
>
> And being hungry, he was desirous to taste something. And as they were preparing, there came upon him an ecstasy of mind;
>
> And he saw the heavens opened, and a certain vessel descending, as it were a great linen sheet let down by the four corners from heaven to the earth.
>
> Wherein were all manner of four-footed beasts, and creeping things of the earth, and fowls of the air.
>
> And there came a voice to him: Arise, Peter, kill, and eat.
>
> But Peter said: Far be it from me; for I never did eat anything that is common and unclean.
>
> And the voice spoke to him again the second time: That which God hath cleansed do not thou call common.
>
> And this was done thrice: and presently the vessel was taken up into heaven.
>
> Now whilst Peter was doubting within himself, what the vision that he had seen should mean: behold the men who were sent from Cornelius, inquiring for Simon's house, stood at the gate.
>
> And when they had called, they asked, if Simon, who is surnamed Peter, were lodged there?
>
> And as Peter was thinking of the vision, the Spirit said to him: Behold three men seek thee.
>
> Arise, therefore, get thee down, and go with them, doubting nothing: for I have sent them.
>
> —Acts x:9–20.

Peter, obedient to the Holy Ghost, accompanied the messengers to Caesarea where he baptized Cornelius and his whole family. For the first time there was in the Church a Gentile who had not passed through the synagogue.

The vision of St. Peter is the divine solution of the irritating problem. Under a most expressive symbolic formula the vision announces that the ancient Law is no longer binding on the Christians, and that consequently one can be a Christian without being a Jew. The Church will not be a Jewish community; it will be an international society where shall meet as brothers, without distinction of rite or race, the Jew and the Gentile, the master and the slave, the poor and the rich. In vain then does Israel promise herself the first place in the kingdom of God. Israel can disappear without causing a vacancy; her mission is ended and her place henceforth will be taken by a spiritual Israel made up of all the faithful.

One will understand the excitement that was stirred up in Jerusalem at news of the baptism in Caesarea. St. Peter was interpellated and had to explain; he made known that he had acted only on the order of the Lord, and his contradictors kept silent. As to the faithful they repeated among themselves: "God then hath also to the gentiles given repentance unto life."

### *Ultra-Jewish Christians still object.*

Accordingly it might seem that all difficulties had been removed and that all discussion, all hesitation had ceased in the Church now that its course had been set right by the hand of God Himself. But this would be to disregard the intensity of doctrinal feeling. Those Christians who put their Jewish patriotism above their Christian faith did not give up their favorite idea concerning the privilege of Israel. This doctrine was part, so to speak, of their flesh and blood; it was one of the constituent elements of their faith; it was identified in their thoughts with the Christian doctrine. They seemed to have let the baptism at Caesarea pass as a miraculous exception, not as a rule. Who knows but that more than one bore a grudge against Peter on account of his vision, looked on him as a dreamer and visionary. In any case, heedless that Peter had spoken, they calmly persevered in their contention that one could not become a Christian without first becoming a naturalized Jew.

Such was the situation when one day there came to Jerusalem news far more serious than that of the baptism of a single family of gentiles. It was told that in Antioch, in that great city which was the queen of the East, some of the faithful were preaching the Gospel to Gentiles and receiving them into communion through baptism without any other initiation. Converting into a rule the exception of Caesarea, they were not imposing the Jewish rite on these new converts, they were not making them observe the fundamental distinction between clean and unclean food, they were dispensing them from all the precepts of the Law, they were surrendering the heritage of Israel to children who did not want Israel as a father. And to make it clear that they meant to inaugurate a new tradition and break with the past, they were taking a name never before in use among the faithful, a name that had been recently coined at Antioch: they were calling themselves Christians!

This time the scandal was great. It was impossible to blind themselves further:- the innovators of Antioch were overthrowing the whole hierarchical order in the relations among nations, they were abolishing the privilege of Israel, and compelling the people of God to mingle henceforth with the crowd of newcomers of every descent who were about to invade the Church. Were these innovators to triumph it would be a seeming abandonment of the Christians of the first hour who formed the nucleus of the faithful and among whom were the most devoted disciples of Christ; to say the least it would be for them a very bitter humiliation.

### *Council of Jerusalem imposes solution.*

All the outraged feelings of patriotism, all the passions of self-love, and, perhaps, also of self-interest, were let loose against the school of Antioch which was but applying the rule of faith established by the Supreme Pontiff. Zealots hurried to the capital of Syria to oppose the propaganda of these disturbers and to persuade the new converts that there was no salvation for them unless to their baptism they added the practice of the Law. But at Antioch the emissaries came in contact with a force they did not know. Paul, the greatest genius of rising Christianity, showed himself in all his power. Sent by the community of Antioch to Jerusalem to explain his position to the apostles, Paul set out with Barnabas for the Holy City and then took place that solemn assembly of the apostles and the disciples, known to historians as the Council of Jerusalem. The momentous question was presented and, as was to be expected, it was decided in the way that Providence itself had pointed out in the vision of Joppe. At this meeting Peter spoke with power and dignity and, indeed, showed himself, to the eyes of all, the infallible head of the Church of God. Stretching out his hand to the Apostle of the nations, he took under his protection the victim of the fanatics, proclaimed his orthodoxy before the whole Church; he sealed with him that fraternal union which time has consecrated into a glorious partnership – making them the household gods of the new Rome. Not less decisive was the attitude of James the Just, the most orthodox and pious of the Jews, on whom all the reactionaries relied, who spoke in accordance with Peter and threw the weight of his unequalled prestige in support of the much disparaged innovations. After the discussion the First Council flung open the doors of the Church to the nations in this sublime declaration: "It hath seemed good to the Holy Ghost and to us, to lay no further burden upon you than the necessary things."

The Council of Jerusalem had saved Christianity, but it had sacrificed Judaism. In deciding that the Church would be Catholic, that is to say, international, it had killed the national pretensions of the Jewish clique. Then ended forever the time-honored dream in which the seers had seen the children of Israel seated on the very steps of the throne whence the Messiah ruled all the nations of the earth. But it was to be a "spiritual Israel," a symbolic Sion that the prophets had announced; strangers were taking the place of the children of the family at the banquet; from the stones by the roadside God was raising up children to Abraham. Thus at last the hidden meaning of the Scripture was revealed. More than one Christian Jew must have said to himself that God was not fulfilling the promise made to Abraham and to Jacob, that He was repelling the people with whom He had an everlasting covenant and that He was covering with shame the daughter of Sion. Many of them, like the captive Hebrews at Babylon, sat and wept bitter tears as they remembered disinherited Sion. "Upon the rivers of Babylon, there we sat and wept: when we remembered Sion." (Ps. CXXXVI, 1) Let us greet with respect this patriotic grief than which there is scarcely any more exalted, but let us not forget that the cause of the Church was superior to that of Israel, and that the interests of humanity go before those of country. Some of the Christian Jews were not resigned. After the Council of Jerusalem, they continued their desperate opposition to the teachings of the Church, to the definitions that she had promulgated, to the apostolate of the Gentiles. Clinging obstinately to the old national prejudices which they identified with orthodoxy, they soon became but a small refractory sect cast upon the road to heresy. The catastrophe in which Jerusalem perished some years later drowned their opposition in a deluge of blood and was, to the Christian Jews, a decisive revelation which came to confirm that of Joppe. After this it was plain that Israel was no longer the people of God, but a rejected nation. It is no longer worth while to fix upon it the attention of history.

*First turning point in Church's history.*

As for the Church, she had just separated her cause from the precarious destiny of a nation. She had refused to espouse the cause of the petty contingencies of history so as not to fail in her universal mission. Peter's bark had cut the rope that bound it to port and was gaining the high seas where, without doubt, there awaited it storms, but also miraculous draughts of fishes. Such was the first turning point in the history of the modern world.

Chapter III

# THE CHURCH AND THE BARBARIANS

*Christianity becomes religion of Roman Empire.*

THENCEFORTH THERE WAS NOTHING TO PREVENT Christianity from becoming the religion of the Roman Empire, that is, of all the nations grouped under the shadow of the Roman civilization. For indeed, what were all the other dangers awaiting the Church compared to the danger which had nearly destroyed her on the threshold of life? The bloody persecutions which marked the three centuries of her early life proved no obstacle to her growth. It is true that the fury of her persecutors spilled the blood of multitudes of her children; but this blood, in accordance with the expression of an apologist, was a seed of marvellous fecundity. After three hundred years of a war of extermination, the Roman Empire had to acknowledge itself conquered by its victim and had to surrender to her its arms. By the edict of Milan, promulgated in 312, Emperor Constantine the Great proclaimed that henceforth all might adore God as they wished. This was recognizing implicitly the right of Christianity to exist. But it is the glorious privilege of the Catholic Church that she needs naught but the common right in order that she may conquer the universe. As soon as liberty of conscience was established, the Roman world in its entirety asked for admission into the communion of the faithful, and before the fourth century had drawn to a close the pagans saw themselves reduced to the state of a discouraged minority. Christianity had become the religion of the emperors, the religion of the provinces; its limits were coextensive with those of the Empire. There were Christian communities on the borders of the Rhine and of the Danube, as well as on the banks of the Euphrates and of the Nile; there were Christian communities in

Colchis as well as in the Isle of Britain; and the Christian religion was sufficiently designated when it was called the Roman religion.

### Christianity linked with Roman civilization.

Thus the humble sect of the Galileans held the throne of the Caesars and its future was linked with the destinies of the *eternal civilization*. Truly, the powerful constitution of the Roman Empire seemed well fitted to last for all time. Such was the universal belief; and never did a patriotic dogma rally more enthusiastic and more sincere adherents than the creed of all Roman citizens, which found expression in those proud words: *the eternity of the Empire!* This formula recurs in the verses of the poets, in the prayers of the faithful, in the panegyrics of the orators, and even in the text of the laws. Rome, in the language of its pagan worshipers, was called the Eternal City, and Christianity, in borrowing this appellation from the civil language, did not wish, at least in the beginning, to modify its traditional sense.

This goes to show that the Christians had adopted without misgiving the common belief in the eternity of the Roman civilization. Whatever the pretensions of their persecutors, the Christians were not less patriotic than the pagans, though in another way, and their religious belief contained nothing contrary to their convictions as citizens. Nay more, they found in their sacred volumes passages which seemed to confirm this conviction in a marvellous manner. For what was that fourth and last empire foretold by Daniel – and compared to iron to symbolize its indestructible duration – but the Roman Empire? This belief in the eternity of the Roman Empire was, in a way, part and parcel of their faith; in fact, it was adduced by the first apologists as an unanswerable proof of their patriotism. "How," said one of them, "could we desire the end of the Empire, since thereby we would desire the end of the world?"

### Barbarians capture Rome.

But dark clouds were gathering slowly on the horizon, disturbing the serenity of the world and announcing the catastrophe of the morrow. The

Barbarians, strangers to Christianity and to civilization, excluded from the *Roman felicity*, were prowling like wolves about the sunny domain of the Empire. Rome, having tried to subdue them, at last came to the conclusion that its hour for new conquests was past and that it would never triumph over them by force of arms. The time came when the Barbarians were supplying her with soldiers and it was among them that she recruited her staunchest defenders. Germany was to antiquity what Switzerland has been to modern Europe:- a land of lansquenets. Every year, crossing the Rhine or the Alps, the warriors of that country came in bands to hire out the work of their muscular arms to the generals of the Empire. Lovers of sunshine, of wealth, of voluptuousness, they came in quest of fortune and sometimes they found the crown. History records the names of some of these adventurers. One was Maximinus, a type of colossal brute, who under Septimus Severus, ran for hours at a time alongside the chariot of the emperor; later he murdered the Emperor Alexander and usurped his throne. Another was Odoacer. We meet him first in history when, on his way to Italy to sell his services to the Empire, he stopped at the entrance of the hut of a far-famed and kindly hermit of Norica, now Bavaria. A barbarian of gigantic stature, he had to stoop to cross the threshold of the hut of the saintly old man whom he wished to greet in passing. A few years later this hireling was king of Italy.

How did the Empire act towards these men whom it could no longer subdue, and of whose services it had incessant need? It concluded that it should rally them to its cause, not by paying them for the blood they would shed for it, but by assimilating them gradually, by making true Romans of them and by handing them over to the Church to make them Christians. This seemed comparatively easy. The Roman civilization was not an exclusive world; it was thrown wide open to any Barbarian who was willing to serve it; and it had sufficient attraction to induce him to exchange his savagery for the Roman life. And in this way, by a sort of tacit agreement, there was worked out the transfusion of the Germanic world into the Roman world:- the former, little by little, took possession of the latter, whilst the latter in turn assimilated the former. It was the peaceful triumph of civilization, superior to all armed conquests. For was it not a triumphant proof of the eternity of the Roman civilization, that a Stilicho[1] and an Aetius[2] gained victories in its name, that a victorious Ataulph[3] proclaimed the grandeur of Rome in penitent accents, that Theodoric the Great[4] continued the work of the Emperors?

In this way the Empire held, towards the Barbarians, the attitude Israel had maintained towards the Gentiles. Rome could form no conception of a community of nations save under the Roman form and with Rome at its head. Allow me another comparison which will present my thought in a more striking manner. The European of today cannot imagine that our modern civilization may perish; it does not occur to him that one day the deep masses of Asiatic people or unorganized hordes of anarchists may destroy it without at the same time unchaining chaos;[5] such an eventuality would be, in his opinion, the end of all social life, the return of mankind to the darkness of primeval savagery. Well then, the Roman of the fourth century had a viewpoint very similar – with just this difference, that, for him, modern civilization was the Roman Empire.

*The Christian Romans see in fall of Rome end of civilization.*

Thus, for the second time, the destinies of the Church were linked with those of a human institution. Just as the Christian Jews were firmly convinced that the future of Christianity was indissolubly united with the future of their own people, so the Christian Romans imagined that their future was one with the future of the Empire. The Empire, indeed, was civilization itself; it was felicity, it was the perfection of social life, and its chief – in the solemn language of that day – bore the title of Prince of the Human Race. Identified with the Empire, the Christian Church, by that very fact, seemed identified with the whole human race. She apparently had attained her ideal, with nothing more to ask of future centuries, and it seemed that it should be her chief concern to preserve the prevailing conditions.

Bearing in mind this universal viewpoint of the Romans, we may imagine their feelings as the trend of events, instead of pointing to the fulfilment of their dreams, seemed, on the contrary, to foreshadow the destruction of the Empire by the Barbarians. Every day they saw increase the number of these hirelings who became their plague. Of gigantic stature, powerful of limb, untidy, red-haired, with unkempt beard, their legs covered with rags, ill-smelling, and, moreover, coarse, brutal, ignorant, talking a hoarse and unintelligible jargon, they spread everywhere, treated the Provinces as their own possession, disregarding wholly the Roman mode of living, taking from it only its pleasures, for the rest holding to their own ways without any intention of change. A day indeed came – a day of shame and of mourning such as the world had never known – when the savage hordes captured the Eternal City. Then was the sanctuary of civilization violated in a most sacrilegious manner; and men had a foretaste of the end of all things!

And indeed to them the end of the Roman civilization was the end of the world. If all that is beautiful in life – style, wealth, well-being, public games, literature, arts, refined social manners – was to be suppressed; and if a flood of barbarism was to be let loose upon a world, radiant, charming, thrilling with the joy of life, would it not mean death to the human race itself? Thus they all said and felt. For to admit for a single moment that the human race could get along without the Roman civilization, and that the future of the former was not indissolubly connected with the prosperity of the latter, was an absurd and impossible thought which no one entertained.

Accordingly, when undeniable signs announced to them the fall of that civilization, the true Romans could but desire death. Some wished to fall in a last intoxication at the banquet of civilization, crowned with roses and drunk with wine; others, wrapped in the folds of the old Roman flag, awaited the blow with stoic despair, even as the senators of yore, seated in their curule chairs, the arrival of the Gallic conqueror. All perished with their ideal, incapable of conceiving any other, witnessing the crash of heaven and of their gods. There are no more tragic sorrows than these, because they touch humanity in those things which it loves and admires the most. All realities may fail so long as the ideal stands; if the ideal also proves false not only is the heart broken, but the mind is shattered, and the intellect casts itself headlong into nothingness with a cry of utter despair.

In similar crises it is with a fresh outburst of fanaticism that the vanquished meet the sentence of destiny. This was particularly the case with the Romans of Britain. Located at the border of the civilized world and abandoned by Rome at an early hour, they saw the Anglo-Saxon invasion spread gradually, pushing them back from day to day towards the West, crushing civilization in the portions of the country they had invaded, and choking it in the rest of the land. Entrenched in their fierce patriotism, no longer understanding anything of the progress of the world, they could but protest. Christians themselves, they were not willing that their conquerors should be called to the blessings of the Gospel, and their priests refused to communicate to the newcomers the light of the Gospel, unwilling as they were to admit that one could be both Christian and Anglo-Saxon, just as the Jews had been unwilling that one should be Christian and uncircumcised. They did not realize that in converting their conquerors they would save themselves; they preferred to perish whilst hating them, rather than to live reconciled with them. It is the eternal cry of fanaticism: – "rather Turk than Papist." The Armenians of today realize the significance of such a wish.

*Catholic Church sees in Barbarian movement birth of new civilization.*
If the Catholic Church had not understood her role better than the Briton clergy, if she had not risen above the resentments of blind patriotism, Christianity would not have survived, but would have sunk into the abyss along with the Roman Empire. But the Church had a steadier eye and a calmer mind; she did not despair of humanity, she did not believe that all was lost because Rome was doomed. She viewed the gigantic movement as a whole, and discovered in it the birth of a world as yet unknown. She foresaw the sublime novelty which then could have been expressed only by a monstrous coupling of words, *the barbarian civilization*, that is, a civilization that could get on without Rome, and which would go farther than Rome. And, undaunted, conscious of her eternal mission, she went to those who were then the heralds of destiny, and, her hand in theirs, she took the road of the future.

I have explained elsewhere the genesis of the movement which was to draw the Catholic Church in this direction:- this movement is identified with the name of the greatest Doctor of the Latin Church, St. Augustine.[6] Let it suffice to state here that this movement, conceived in the thought of a man of genius and nurtured by his disciples, found, from the end of the fifth century, laborers who carried it from the purely intellectual domain into that of historical realities. On the one hand, the Gallic episcopacy represented by men like St. Remigius of Rheims and St. Avitus of Vienne, sincerely adherent to the domination of the Barbarians, asked them only to become Christians, and thus bravely renounced the chimerical dream of continuing the Roman civilization. On the other hand, the Papacy, in the person of the greatest man of the sixth century, St. Gregory the Great, took the initiative in the conversion of the Anglo-Saxons, thus fulfilling, from his palace in Rome, the task which the Celtic Church of Britain had disdained to assume. Everywhere, without imposing conditions, the Catholic Church unlocked the gates of her sanctuaries and opened the road of salvation to the new nations. Thus is explained her prodigious success during the sixth century with all the Barbarians, whether Arian[7] or pagan. When these became convinced that they could carry the sweet yoke of Christ without submitting to the heavy yoke of Rome, their prejudices against the Catholic Faith fell to the ground, and its natural superiority over heresy, as well as over paganism, found no longer any obstacle. Joyfully the Barbarian world, whole and entire, entered into the Church. The peoples became converted as a whole. In less than three centuries all the Germanic nations were won over to Catholicism. More time had been required to convert the Empire, notwithstanding the enormously superior advantages it offered to the apostolate.

### *The second turning point in Church's history.*

We have now passed the second turning point of history, which was inaugurated by the baptism of Clovis.[8] This baptism has often been compared to that of Constantine.[9] I would say that it matches, in a remarkable way, the baptism of the centurion Cornelius. Then, the Church, separating her cause from that of the people of Israel, had gone to the nations and had received them into the Christian community without imposing upon them the obligations of the Judaic Law. This time, detaching her destinies from those of the Empire, she went to the Barbarians and put into their hands the scepter of the world without requiring them to wear the dress of the Roman civilization. On both occasions, it was a stroke of strategy of the same superior order. On both occasions, Christianity, the common patrimony of all humanity, had escaped utter destruction. Instead of weeping on the graves of extinct civilizations, Christianity had busied herself with winning to the faith of Christ the nascent communities. She had thus indicated in a precise and explicit manner, and for all centuries to come, that, as she is created to spread the kingdom of God on earth, she cannot identify herself with any of those ephemeral things which are called dynasty, nation, social class, civilization. Having become the universal religion at this price, it is at this price also that she will remain such and continue to make a reality of that sublime epithet given to the Messiah: *the Father of the world to come.*

CHAPTER IV

# THE CHURCH AND FEUDALISM

LETTING THE DEAD BURY THEIR DEAD, LETTING CRUMBLE behind her the moldering edifice of Roman civilization, the Catholic Church, true to her mission, went to the Barbarians and confided to them her destiny. Established in their midst, she chose from them co-laborers, such as St. Boniface,[10] Charlemagne,[11] Alfred the Great,[12] and from the very first set herself to the task of bringing forth a new world.

It was a gigantic project, a work of centuries. It would be inspiring and profitable to consider the undertaking in detail; but this is not the place to trace a sketch of it – that I have done elsewhere.[13] My aim is rather to show how, in the course of her work, the Church was in danger of falling victim to the Barbarian she sought to civilize, and how she finally succeeded in her task.

*Generosity of Barbarians to Church.*

One must realize what kind of men were these new peoples, who had just bowed their heads under the waters of baptism, in the first centuries of the Middle Ages. With the exception of a few chosen ones, they were still only on the threshold of Christianity and, though baptized, were far from being civilized. They sincerely loved the Christian religion, but their love for it was often crude and sordid. In their eyes, there were two ways for a disciple of Christ to give proof of his faith: to deal vigorous blows to its enemies, and to make large benefactions to its poor. It was their belief – as it is ours – that *charity covers a multitude of sins*. And as they had many sins to be forgiven, they showed themselves very generous towards the Church. Nothing more meritorious. The Church was the mother and the nurse of the poor. To give to her was not only to contribute to the maintenance of worship and to the needs of the active ministry, it was to assure the budget of charity and of public instruction of which the Church had the sole charge. Behold how, "for the salvation of their souls and for the remission of their sins," as they loved to state in their acts of donation, the men of that time were pleased to endow religious institutions or to found new ones. There was not a monastery, there was not a cathedral or collegiate church which had not received largesses at their hands and which they had not made, in a short time, owner of valuable property, invested with all the social prestige which rich estates gave in those days. More than one of these establishments became in this manner a real power, especially from the days when kings, outdoing the nobles in their liberality, actually divided their authority with the Church and granted her in fief entire counties, with all the political and civil rights, and made her prelates temporal princes, the first personages of the state after themselves. Europe became covered with ecclesiastical principalities, veritable buttresses of the thrones which had created them.

### *Secular interference with Church affairs.*

But so much wealth and prestige, far from being a real power, became on the contrary a supreme danger to the Church. I do not speak here of the violences pure and simple of the depredators, which were, after all, incontestable crimes against right and public order. There is question of a more universal and deeper evil. At once opulent and unarmed the Church was obliged to confide to lay hands the sword which the State had given her; and because she lacked an hereditary dynasty she was subject to all kinds of rivalry whenever a benefice became vacant. Thus the Church very soon became the plaything of the ambitious and the prey of rival factions. Even those who, in their hours of recollection or repentance, had shown themselves the most generous towards her, did not hesitate to dispose of her dignities, persuading themselves that the liberalities they had bestowed upon her gave them a right of tutelage or protectorate over her. All the great ones were on the watch at the deathbeds of bishops or abbots to contend for the vacant inheritance. Having cadets to place and not wishing to endow them with their own possessions, lest they should reduce the share of the eldest son, they conceived the idea of putting the burden of their support on the shoulders of the Church, by making them bishops or abbots. The ecclesiastical hierarchy thus became a dumping ground for numerous families and the Church became, in a way, an institution of employment for the cadets of good families.

On the other hand it was to the interest of kings that ecclesiastical dignities should be given only to reliable and faithful persons. In feudal society the political influence acquired by dioceses and monasteries was too important to leave kings indifferent to the recruitment of the hierarchy. Again these rich grants were for them excellent means of government, which they used to reward the fidelity of some, to stimulate the zeal of others. They were not slow, then, contrary to the canons of the Church, in acquiring almost everywhere the habit of personally selecting the titularies of the principal ecclesiastical dignities in their kingdom. The kings of Germany did more: they arrogated to themselves, towards the middle of the tenth century, the nomination of the Sovereign Pontiffs, so that during about a hundred years (963 – 1073) no pope could ascend the see of Peter who had not been designated or at least agreed on by them.

We should inspect this regime at range. When a bishop died, his chapter at once took possession of the insignia of his priestly dignity:- the ring, which represents his marriage to his diocese, and the crosier, which is the symbol of his authority over his flock, and sent them to the king! But no matter how the messengers hastened on their errand, they were preceded by other travellers quicker than themselves; these were the ambitious ones who dreamed of settling in the vacant chair and who had hurried to the royal court to plead their cause. This was the *steeple-chase* of candidates for the episcopacy. I leave it to the reader to imagine the numberless intrigues, wire-pullings, solicitations, promises, enticing offers made to the more influential courtiers, the selling of influence to the highest bidder, the extraordinary interventions which took place. All this scheming was kept up until they learned that the monarch had made his selection. The lucky candidate was then sent for, and, in a distinctively feudal ceremony, received at the hands of the king the crosier and the ring. There was no longer anything canonical in the whole procedure, there was no longer anything ecclesiastical in the ceremony; the investiture, that is to say, the act by which the new bishop was supposed to be endowed with his powers, was exclusively a lay ceremony.

### *Lay investiture.*

Bear in mind this word *lay investiture* – it was to become famous in history; it was to be the watchword of the regime. And, meanwhile, note also the character of the relations which henceforth were to exist between Church and State. The great evangelical principle of the distinction of the powers, which is the cornerstone of modern civilization, was violated in the most flagrant manner. The spiritual and temporal were confounded. No longer was there rendered to God what belonged to God. It would seem that it was the emperor, and no longer the pope, who was Vicar of Jesus Christ. The Church was thus but an annex to the state; the feudal system had enriched her, but it had also enslaved her. It had stripped her of her ecumenical character to make her an institution of caste. The pope was nothing but an imperial chaplain. The bishops were but court chaplains:- the hierarchy was open only to the scions of great families. There arose an ecclesiastical feudalism as there was a military feudalism – both recruited from the same class. The Church leaned upon the powerful ones of the world; she shared their wealth and their authority; it would seem that her destinies were linked indissolubly to those of feudalism. One might say that like the people of Israel, like the Roman Empire, feudalism had wished to dominate the Church, and that, more fortunate than these, it had succeeded.

### *Evil results of lay investiture.*

This situation was grave beyond precedent, both for the welfare of the Church herself and for her influence upon the nations. From the moment the choice of prelates, instead of being regulated by rigorous canonical prescriptions, depended solely on the arbitrary power of the kings, it was no longer priestly virtue which opened the ranks of the episcopate. The great question was to give to the sovereign guarantees of fidelity to his dynasty and to his politics, or to be endorsed by his courtiers. But the courtiers no longer gave their protection gratuitously;

they sold it. Most of the bishops, therefore, bought their office, and, naturally, once they had acquired it, they endeavored to indemnify themselves by selling in their turn the dignities of secondary order. The inferior clergy, on their side, in order to reimburse themselves, sold the sacraments, and in this manner, from the top to the bottom of the ladder, the grace of the redemption was sold at auction. The temple of God out of which Jesus had driven the sellers had become a den of thieves.

But, of all abuses, this kind of traffic was the one the Church condemned the most severely, and the one against which she had formulated most of her anathemas. From the dawn of Christianity, she had indignantly stigmatized it – from the day when Simon the magician offered money to St. Peter to obtain the power of imposition of hands, and drew from the Prince of the Apostles this thundering reply: "Keep thy money to thyself to perish with thee!" (Acts VIII, 20) From that day on the name of simony has been given to traffic in sacred things, and all generations have renewed the prohibition of this sacrilegious practice.

And, of course, a simoniacal clergy did not worry much about the virtues of its vocation. Having entered Holy Orders, for the most part, in order to obtain a suitable position, they enjoyed the good things of life, indulged in high living, took part in all worldly distractions, festivities, games, hunting, and even war. A very large number of priests showed their love for the sacraments by receiving two that are incompatible: Holy Orders and Matrimony! They lived openly as fathers of families, surrounded by their wives and children, and they considered celibacy an antiquated custom no longer to be observed. Needless to say these pretended marriages, forbidden by canon law, were in the eyes of the Church nothing but shameful concubinages.

You may imagine the influence which a clergy so degraded could exert upon the people whom it was their duty to instruct and uplift. The most powerful of all teaching is example:- but their example taught the people to trample under foot, with cynicism or without conscience, the most formal precepts of the religion of which they were the ministers. We who, by the grace of God, live in a time when the clergy, by the admirable dignity of their lives, bear testimony to the truth of their teachings, can hardly imagine the sad condition of the faithful of those days, who saw the priesthood invaded by men who lived in concubinage and who were traffickers in the sacraments. When luxury and venality had their seats in the sanctuary and talked from the pulpits, what could be the feelings of the hearers? Christ said to His first priests: "You are the salt of the earth. But if the salt lose its savor, wherewith shall it be salted?" These words found a sad application in the society of those days. Social progress had come to a standstill, and the Christian world went backwards. Some of the faithful – and these the more barbarous – quietly followed in the footsteps of their pastors and plunged into the mire of all vices; others – and these the more logical – turned away with disgust from a religion which they saw represented by such ministers. Both classes were, so to say, ripe for a religious revolution which would have snatched them away from the influence of Christianity. Heresy could confidently knock at their door: – it was sure to find admission.

*Albigensian heresy.*

And indeed, from the beginning of the eleventh century we see heresy everywhere – and such heresy! A doctrine disastrous, lugubrious, horrible as sin and as death! A dark night which came down with the weight of lead and with the coldness of ice upon the mind and upon the heart, a chancre of death which ate at all the luminous and elevated faculties of the human soul, a deadly folly that choked the joy of living and made existence here below like a bad dream:- such was the heresy of the Albigenses! Compare it not to any other heresy:- all others left standing the sacred banner of hope, kept the faith in Christ the Redeemer, maintained in the souls of men the high and manly conviction that life is worth living, that the struggle between good and evil will finally close in keeping with the demands of human conscience. According to the Albigensian heresy, on the contrary, there was certainty of salvation, neither through the Church which they held worthy of all contempt, nor through the Redeemer who according to them had been subject to the law of sin, nor through the law of God who in their opinion was not almighty, but opposed by an evil principle whose power equalled His own. Instead of the harmony, the equilibrium, the order, which the Christian faith sees in the rule of the Divine Wisdom throughout the universe, the Albigensian perceived nothing but an atrocious struggle

# THE CHURCH AND FEUDALISM

between good and evil, fighting for possession of the world in a duel, whose tragic stake was the soul of man.

The Albigensian held that the Christian faith was vain and the Redemption but a lure: that evil was an eternal principle and that the created world, with all its splendors, was its work. He maintained that it was man's own fault if he was composed of a soul and a body – the soul the work of the good god, and the body the work of the evil god. The soul, he said, had been lured into the body by the seductions of the evil god; it was imprisoned there, and its only hope of salvation was to leave it at any cost. Hence suicide was a religious act, since it liberated the soul; hence marriage was to be disapproved because, by reproduction, it perpetuated indefinitely the captivity of souls in the bodies. One sees here collective suicide, the monstrous tenet of a modern philosophy, vaguely advocated as the only solution.

Such were the leading features of the pernicious doctrine which dried up the supernatural life of humanity at its source and plunged the human conscience into the dread darkness whence Christ had called it unto the light of the Redemption. Alas, the men of that epoch must have felt sorely forsaken, sorely disabused of the Christian ideal or they would not, in their despair, have cast themselves in so large numbers into the arms of such a religion! And yet day by day it spread wider and wider. Like one of those deadly scourges which in the past came from Asia, it advanced little by little: the historian can follow on the map the progress of its itinerary of death covering every land as with a pall.

It is called the Albigensian heresy, and we know for a fact that at a certain moment its principle forces were concentrated about Albi in the South of France. But have no illusion on the subject:- it was everywhere. It was in the north, at Arras, at Liège and in the center of France, at Chalons, at Orleans, that it exhibited its most ancient manifestations. Hidden often under the most inoffensive exterior, it was difficult to recognize it at first sight in any particular sect; of harmless appearance, as in the case of the earlier Waldenses[14] it gradually and fatally invaded all centers where the disappearance of Catholic faith had left a void, and legions of men lived under its shadow, never realizing that the mutilated Christianity of which they made profession was but a branch of the Manichean trunk. All the sects of that time were like so many lateral canals which discharged their waters into the central sewer of Manicheism.[15] Directly or indirectly, all the other heresies were its tributaries. They swarmed everywhere. A thousand extravagant and scandalous sects sprang into existence, hideous vermin which covered the poor sick body of society. Among a populace on the verge of frenzy, but still feeling the need of religion, the fiercest of heresiarchs, the vilest of charlatans found a welcome and a hearing. As proof of this I mention the wretch, Tanchelm, who had chosen the city of Antwerp as his field of operation. Such was the fanatical enthusiasm of his followers that – excuse the repugnant detail – they went the length of drinking the water in which he had washed himself. One day he announced that he was going to marry the Blessed Virgin and that he had placed an offering box on either side of the door at the house where the ceremony was to take place; he wished to know – from the liberality they would show in filling them – which of his followers, men or women, were the more devoted to him. Both boxes were filled.

If, as I have said a while ago, it is not always easy to detect the hidden relationship which connected all the sects of the time with the leading heresy, there was nevertheless a very apparent family trait among them all; and that was their boundless aversion for the clergy. And this brings us back, by a roundabout way that has not failed to be instructive, to the origin which I have assigned to this dreadful inundation of heresy:- the corruption of the clergy. It was the scandal of simoniacal and concubinary priests that opened the door through which the multitudes rushed headlong out of the Church.

*Restoration of Christian spirit among clergy.*

It might have seemed, accordingly, that Christianity and civilization were running into bankruptcy. But the Catholic Church is made for eternal renewals. Sometimes it might appear that the sources of grace and of life coming down upon her from the heavenly heights lose themselves and run waste in the distance; but, no! – at a given moment they gush forth from her bosom in columns so much the higher for having been buried the deeper, to spread about her in refreshing and life-giving streams. And this was what men actually saw in those dark days. The inexhaustible vitality of the Church, under the impure flood of heresy, withdrew and concentrated towards her heart; there she drew a greater intensity and energy, and prepared to enter by vigorous pulsations into all the arteries and veins of this great suffering body.

Meanwhile she lived a refugee in the cloisters – those perpetual asylums of the persecuted Christian spirit. All the cloisters had not remained equally free from corruption, but, from the beginning of the tenth century, an active reform movement had originated in those of Lorraine and of Burgundy. Reformers had appeared who had dreamed of restoring to monastic life all its ideal perfection and who succeeded in their efforts. Thus at Gorze, at Brogne, at Cluny especially, there were centers of monastic reform and regeneration whose activities radiated into the distance. Cluny, which had the good fortune to have at its head for more than a century a succession of eminent men, has left its name to this movement. The disciples and the admirers of the Cluniac school carried its ideas and its reform into all the lands of Western Europe. To be just, one must note also the part in the work of reform due to the illustrious Italian ascetics, such as St. Romuald, the founder of the Camaldolese, St. John Gualbert, the founder of Vallombrosa, St. Nilus, who won over to the attraction of the religious life the Emperor Otho III himself, and who, perhaps, might have induced him to lay down the crown if death had not freed the young prince from this heavy burden.

All these monastic hearths, shining forth one after another like the stars of heaven, preserved and fed the sacred fire of the Christian spirit; they restored an atmosphere where all those who had held to the ideal of the Gospel and who had not despaired of the future gathered to refresh themselves. The ranks of the militant church were formed anew about the monasteries; the secular clergy, in turn, furnished doctors and advocates to the cause of the reform. Such was the magnanimous Wazon, Bishop of Liège, the first to define with absolute precision the principles which have been called Gregorian, but which it would suffice to call Catholic. Such again was the noble Anselm of Lucca, the great and exemplary bishop, who became pope under the name Alexander II, and who was destined to be one of the most deserving of the precursors of Gregory VII.[16] And there were many others. They all had their eyes fixed on the Roman See; over the heads of the corrupt episcopacy, all asked of the pope the salvation of the world. To use the modern expression, they were ultramontane in the fullest sense of the word.

### *Reforms demanded.*

These men, scattered everywhere, lent the prestige of a life above reproach to elevated and pure doctrines; and little by little, they compelled public interest; it may be said that they formed public opinion in the centers where religious and social problems were discussed. Their activities were not confined to the ranks of the clergy; they recruited adherents from all classes of society, even from among the princes and the crowned heads. One of them was the powerful Emperor of Germany, Henry III, the pitiless opponent of simony and Nicolaitanism. No one has branded those abuses with more bitterness, no one has fought them with more vigor. He took care to entrust episcopal sees only to men above reproach, and those whom his influence raised to the chair of Peter – Clement II and Damasus II – were worthy of it beyond contradiction. This may seem strange on the part of a sovereign who more than any other held to his pretended right of lay investiture; but it is easy to explain. In human society, it is one thing to notice an abuse, and another thing to detect its source. The observations which we make at a distance – in the light of history and with all the documentary evidence under our eyes – could not have been made with the same facility by the people who lived in those days – who were in the midst of the fray, who saw only a portion of the facts and who, moreover, were inclined, by self-interest and by their condition in life, to see these facts in a different light. This is why there were in those days – as there are now – good people who, though lamenting the abuses of society, would have indignantly rejected the remedy, had it been proposed to them.

### *Difficulty of situation.*

What was this remedy? As I have said before, it did not consist in the prohibition pure and simple of simony and concubinage. As long as they handed over episcopal sees to men given to simony and concubinage, their vices would occupy the sees with them. The true remedy was to prevent such men from penetrating by stratagem into the fold, from entering, as the saying is, otherwise than by the door. To this end it was necessary again to put in force the canonical prescriptions concerning the election of Church dignitaries; in other words, it was necessary to restore to the Church her liberty and to respect the distinction of the two powers by taking from the kings the power of investiture. This was very simple – it is the very simplicity of the idea that made it dreadful and made it appear chimerical. To deny to princes a privilege to which clung the best as well as the worst, would have let loose the most terrible of wars, a war which Christian society had not known to that day – the war between Church and State. And this war would have been not only a war against the kings but also a struggle against the feudal class, against all that rich and powerful society which supported and favored the Church in its own way, and without which it seemed that she would be doomed to absolute powerlessness. It would have provoked among the hierarchy itself a furious and desperate resistance on the part of all the prelates who owed their dignity to lay investiture and whose titles to possession would have become imperilled by the anathema cast upon their origin. These were frightful anticipations which of necessity disturbed the minds of the reformers. And it is not astonishing that more than one recoiled before such eventualities.

*Tact of Leo IX and successors.*

Nevertheless the Catholic Church did not hesitate. But with what tact, with what prudence, with what caution did she proceed at first! To proclaim the true principles and to insist upon their application would have been useless, since they were not known; and it would have been dangerous, since they were not recognized. She did better:- little by little she re-accustomed the minds of the people to respect those principles, by affirming tacitly the right through precedents which she created when she had the power to do so, making those principles prevail, without show, indeed, but with all the more vigor. An example will show how this reform proceeded.

In 1048, the pontifical throne became vacant and the emperor Henry III designated as its incumbent his cousin Bruno, who was then bishop of Toul and who is known in history as Leo IX. He belonged to that group of zealous and fervent Christians who dreamed of the regeneration of the Church. He did not protest against his selection; he did not say to his cousin's face that he had not the right to dispose of the chair of Peter, and that he, as a bishop, could not consider himself pope except he were elected by the clergy of Rome in accordance with the rules of Canon Law. Such language would have spoiled it all:- Henry III angered, would have named another pope, who, probably, would have been more compliant and the great work of the reform would not have taken place. But what Leo IX did not express in words, he proclaimed through his conduct with not less power, and with more gentleness than if he had spoken. He at once set out to take possession of the pontifical see, but he left as a simple pilgrim, without retinue, staff in hand, praying and fasting on the way; he walked into Rome barefooted and it was only after he had been elected in accordance with the rules of Canon Law that he donned the pontifical insignia and acted as the head of the Church. Thus lay investiture was quietly weakened by the very person who received it, and this without the least conflict. The two successors of Leo IX conformed to his example, and, after a few years, the idea of the liberty of the Apostolic See became so much a matter of course that, in 1059, Pope Nicholas II could take a further step and publish his celebrated constitution on the election of sovereign pontiffs.

### *Nicholas II regulates election of sovereign pontiffs.*

This constitution was a model of energy and cleverness. On the one hand it loudly proclaimed the law and decreed that the pope should be elected by the college of cardinals; on the other hand, it wisely took cognizance of the facts and decided that the ruling emperor, and each of his successors to whom the Church would grant the privilege, should have the right to confirm the election. This concession – intended solely to take care of the transition period – soon fell into disuse, and the constitution of 1059 alone remained in force. It may be fitting to remark here that its dispositions are still in force; it was in accordance with them that the present Pope – Benedict XV – was elected and that his successor will be elected. All will admit that an electoral law which lasts for eight and a half centuries is a rather rare phenomenon of longevity, and one which it would be difficult to find outside of the Catholic Church.

*Gregory VII proscribes lay investiture.*

Thus was the Papacy emancipated; it then put itself to the task of liberating the Church. This is its traditional mission, in accordance with the word spoken to Peter: "but thou being converted confirm thy brethren." All eyes were turned towards the Sovereign Pontiff; having seen him set free, the Christian world then asked him to act. From the bosom of the Church there arose weighty voices begging him to save society. St. Peter Damian, in a way, echoed them all. Dreadful hour! Painful hesitation! Would the Papacy rise to the occasion? Would it dare look the all powerful evil in the face, and, having viewed it from all angles, strike it down? Would it dare pronounce the supreme word which, once spoken, could not be revoked, the word which would be the signal for the universal conflagration? This question was asked at the moment when there had just ascended the Chair of Peter one who had been the soul of all reforms for a generation. He was known then as the Monk Hildebrand; today he is known as Pope Gregory VII. He stood there, on the border line between the past and the future, a man who separates the centuries. He stood ready, lance in hand, knowing that his action would be answered by a thousand confused and terrible cries – the noise either of a falling or of a resurgent world.

I imagine that when Pope Gregory was about to deliver the supreme stroke, he felt his hand tremble. This intrepid reformer – perhaps the most intrepid of men – must then have felt that sacred terror and weakening of the flesh which was not spared Jesus Himself in the Garden of Olives. There is nothing more august and more touching than the voluntary sacrifice made by those whom God has chosen to execute a great mission; they are conscious that they are to be its first victims, but nevertheless they act. Thus, when in 1075 Gregory VII formulated against lay investiture the prohibition which he accentuated in 1078 and in 1080, and when he forbade even kings and emperors to confer any religious dignity, he attained the acme of moral grandeur in his whole career. Never, neither in the passing éclat of his triumph, nor in the magnanimous patience displayed amid the tribulations of his exile, did Gregory VII do anything more sublime than when he made this proclamation, which was about to plunge him into the abyss of endless trouble.

The war which was then kindled lasted fifty years, and neither Gregory VII nor Henry IV lived to see its end. I need not tell you its story – you will find its details in the text books of history; my task is to make you realize its bearing. It was a furious struggle, in which were engaged all Christian peoples, all classes of society. It deeply disturbed a world still young and passionate. It set loose an avalanche of pamphlets in which everything was attacked with a violence theretofore unknown in doctrinal debate. In the course of the conflict there were strange surrenders and strange and sudden changes, and shameful waverings in the most manly characters. The good cause, attacked with unprecedented fury, was often compromised by the extreme measures of its own defenders, and the revolutionary spirit was aided, more than once, by appearing to operate under the auspices of authority. And, in such encounters, the distracted conservatives could turn in anger to the Sovereign Pontiff, and say to him: "Behold your partisans, and behold your work!"

And, as often happens, they unscrupulously identified the reformers with the revolutionaries. As an instance of this we may cite that generous Catholic democracy of Milan, which was guided by St. Arialdo and St. Erlembaldo, but which was branded by its opponents with the name of Cathari – a name, however, which it transformed into a title of honor. The storm which disturbed everything seemed to bring darkness into the minds of men and decadence into Christian society. The Papacy, however, remained undisturbed in the midst of the universal upheaval. Gregory VII died at Salerno, Victor III fled from Rome on the day of his consecration, Urban II prepared the first crusade in the midst of his struggles, Pascal II languished in the prisons of Henry V; but the Papacy, looking beneath the convulsions of the surface, saw arising the harvests of the future. Under the wind of the storm the truths which it had sown grew up in the conscience of the nations. The vital principles of Christianity little by little unfolded their conclusions in formulas of luminous and energetic precision, and slowly succeeded in taking possession of men's minds. Leaning upon the elite of the regular and secular clergy, upheld by the ever growing adherence of the multitudes, served by pure devotedness – such as that of the Countess Mathilda of Tuscany,[17] known as the Joan of Arc of the Papacy – the Holy See held firm.

### *Gregory VII triumphs.*

In fact, thirty-seven years after his death, Gregory VII triumphed from the depth of his grave. In the Concordat of Worms, in 1122, the Church compelled the state to recognize the right for which she had fought so hard. The state gave back to her the freedom of her canonical elections, from that of the pope down to the elections of all the inferior dignitaries; the Church remained sovereign in her domain. In mixed questions she made concessions in accordance with her custom.

Free thenceforth to devote herself entirely to the great work of reform, she displayed an energy and an activity without limit. In less than a century, she extinguished Manicheism; she sent all Europe to the Crusades; she drew forth from her bosom three new orders, the first for the ministry of souls,[18] the second for the preaching of doctrine,[19] the third for the practice of poverty.[20] She presided at the birth of communes and universities, she covered with her prestige Gothic art[21] and scholasticism,[22] she saw saints ascend the thrones of France[23] and of Castile.[24] And, during two centuries, the twelfth and thirteenth, she became the supreme authority of Western Europe, the oracle of the Christian world.

### *A turning point in history of Church.*

Such were the results of the generous reaction whereby the Catholic Church saved her future. To do this she had to tear herself away from the embrace of feudalism, which desired to make of her a religion of camp chapels and connect her with its fleeting destinies. In comparing the Christian Church as it was at the eve of the conflict with what it has been since, one can realize the bearing of this great phenomenon and understand that there is no exaggeration in seeing in this salutary crisis one of the turning points of the history of civilization.

Chapter V

# THE CHURCH AND NEO-CAESARISM

THE CHURCH EMERGED VICTORIOUS FROM THE CONFLICT of the Investitures. Being now free from the abuses which had dishonored her she attained unwonted prestige. The Papacy was like the sun at its zenith: supreme arbiter of the moral and religious life of the peoples; there was no social interest which was foreign to Rome.

### *The Church at her zenith.*

How did the Church use her influence? She had a twofold aim: to pacify Europe and to turn her united forces against Islam. The Popes pursued this sublime ideal with magnificent courage and abnegation. Peace among the Christian peoples was their constant care, just as peace among the individuals had been the special concern of the bishops who, in the tenth and the eleventh centuries, succeeded in establishing the Truce of God.[25] It was also a truce of God of which the Papacy dreamed – no longer a truce between individuals, but a truce between nations. The Papacy desired this truce, in the first place, for the thing itself, since human civilization has no higher aim than peace. She desired it, in the second place, that she might oppose a compact and united Europe against the eternal enemy – the Crescent.[26] And note well, this dream of the Popes of the Middle Ages has remained the inheritance of generous minds, from Joan of Arc and Christopher Columbus down to Leibnitz and Cardinal Lavigerie. And we may hope that it will also be the ideal of Europe, when a re-christianized Europe will have become reconciled with the ideal.

## THE CHURCH AND NEO-CAESARISM

The splendor of the social role of the Papacy at this epoch found majestic expression during the festivities of the First Jubilee, which was celebrated in Rome, in 1300, whilst Boniface VIII occupied the chair of Peter. During the course of that year, the Pope, from the windows of his palace, saw the Christian world pass before him, going to the tombs of the Apostles in order to gain the indulgences of the Jubilee. The Eternal City then presented an incredible spectacle:- there were never fewer than two hundred thousand visitors, a truly astounding number if we consider the primitive modes of travel of those days. An eyewitness has described for us, in immortal verse, these vast throngs crossing the bridge of St. Angelo on their way to and from the Vatican; those going held the right, those coming back the left, as is done at the present day on the bridges of the large German cities. And painting, as well as poetry, has immortalized this spectacle, for one of the most ancient paintings of Giotto – which may be seen to the present day in the Church of St. John Lateran – is his Boniface VIII proclaiming the Jubilee from the loggia of that sanctuary. Certainly in this year of boundless enthusiasm, when the Pope almost seemed to be more than a mere man and saw the whole of mankind at his feet, he needed an act of profound humility to resist the suggestions of such high fortune; more than once he had need to recall the words pronounced on the day of his coronation whilst they burned the tow at the foot of the Pontifical throne: "Holy Father, thus passeth the glory of this world."

*Rule of Christian society wrested from Pope by Lay State.*

And indeed, thus passed the glory of this world for Boniface VIII. Before his death, this old man, at the age of seventy-seven, had to assist at the catastrophe which threatened to engulf the incomparable destinies of the Papacy. Two years after the triumph of the great Jubilee, the mercenaries of the Most Christian King seized the Vicar of Christ in his own palace, and the nation which called herself the eldest daughter of the Church attempted to crush the Roman See. The Pope, when on the brink of the grave, overwhelmed with sorrow and humiliation, knew that a dreadful revolution was consummated, or at least that its principle had been triumphantly affirmed, and that, for centuries to come, the rule of human society had been wrested from the Vicar of Jesus Christ.[27]

Who then was the mysterious and terrible enemy that was about to upset Christian Europe, paralyze the action of the Papacy and the course of civilization? It was the Lay State, a new and conquering power which preceding centuries had not known. It rose suddenly, like a giant, to face the Papacy and provoke it to mortal combat. Armed from the beginning with a theory from which it deduced its omnipotence, this Lay State claimed the adherence of its followers with the authority of an unquestionable dogma, though in reality it had no other principle than force; it began against the Church of Christ the long drawn out combat which has not yet neared its end, and whose fluctuating fortunes remained for our descendants the most solemn problem of history.

*Limited authority of kings becomes absolute.*

This gives me occasion once more to recall that it is ideas which rule the world. It is in the incorporeal region of the mind that are worked out those irresistible forces which destroy or build up:- as yonder, on the silent and solitary summits of the Alps, are formed the streams which flow down to the valleys, to bring them life, when their course is tranquil, but to work devastation, when swollen by the storms.

Let us, in turn, go up to the summits, to discover how, in the region of ideas, there was worked out the political doctrine which was about to fall like an avalanche on this growing society. At first sight, this theory seems opposed to the spirit of the Middle Ages. To the men of this epoch, the king was without doubt the head of society, and religion invested him with a sacred and inviolable character. But his authority was far from being unlimited; everywhere – in the stronghold of the nobleman, in the walled enclosure of the communes, under the vaults of the churches and monasteries, on the lofty throne of St. Peter – it met free forces which acted as a counterpoise and did not permit the king to exceed the limits established by religion and by custom. The king of the Middle Ages was what would today be termed a constitutional king, not that there always existed written documents which formally limited his power, but because the privileges of the various classes of society were, in effect, a limit which he might not overstep, if he did not wish to bear the voice of public anger grumbling about his throne.

If this was the case, how could the idea of royal absolutism, at a given moment, take hold of the minds of men and finally triumph to such a point that it eliminated from modern politics the influence of the Church and of its Head? The question is very complex: I will endeavor, nevertheless, to answer it with clearness and precision.

### *Royal absolutism due to ultra-nationalism and adoption of Roman Law.*

Manifestly, there is among modern peoples – to some extent among all peoples – an invincible repugnance to international governments. Each nation seeks within itself the sovereign principle of its activity; it obeys with pleasure only the authorities which have emanated from its bosom; it is tempted to regard as a stranger a master living at too great a distance. If by their sacred character, by the necessary universality which is part of dogma itself, the religious institutions escape this centrifugal tendency, this is not true of political institutions which nations will not support except on condition that they have them under full control. This explains the dismemberment of the empire of Charlemagne, which was regretted by only a few cultured minds. We may thus understand why for centuries Italy opposed the authority of its emperors. These national tendencies, however little they were excited, became passions, and when aroused by an interested power, these passions knew no bounds. "The Pope or the King, which is to be the ruler of the kingdom of France?" The query, thus put, could receive but one answer, and the best Christians, questioned in this way, sided spontaneously with the king and espoused his cause against the Chief of Christendom, for the defense of the national liberties. To this influence of national self-love, whose power it would be difficult to exaggerate, there was added another force which was not less powerful. At this time all intellectual and scientific superiority was not confined to the ranks of the clergy. A lay society had come into existence and had developed; it had its superior minds, its scientists, its jurists, its statesmen; it was conscious of its power and of its dignity; it took its place alongside of the ecclesiastical order, it had no intention of leaving to the latter the exclusive direction of minds, and already it had taken a prominent part in politics and legislation.

Thus nationalism, on the one part, laicism, on the other part, without being hostile in principle to the Church, had nevertheless a different ideal and pursued a course which was easily set against the aims of the Church. But this opposition, in order to become conscious and intense, needed to be stirred up by some resolute agent; this agent was at hand. We shall see him at work.

The Middle Ages had at all times a strong predilection for the study of antiquity. They put all the more ardor into the study because antiquity was, at this epoch, almost the only object of scientific knowledge. This study gave them an opportunity of knowing another society, a civilization different from theirs. This society appeared to them through the radiant prism of its masterpieces, with the magical colors of a better world. Thus the poets and philosophers of antiquity enjoyed, during the Middle Ages, an authority second only to that of the Gospel. Aristotle[28] was the fetish of the school, the master of those who know, and when his authority had been invoked – *Magister dixit* – the last word had been spoken. As to Virgil – it did not suffice to honor him as the prince of poets; he had become a marvellous personage, half magician, half prophet. Sometimes, this infatuation literally turned the heads of people, as happened in the case of that poor monk of the tenth century who, six hundred years before Don Quixote, took for realities the fictions of Virgil and taught that the only true religion was that of the *Aeneid*![29]

Nowhere did this fetishism for antiquity manifest itself in more extravagant ways and nowhere did it produce more disastrous results than among the men given to the study of law, the jurists, as they were called. I shall confine myself to just one example of this intellectual malady. In accordance with the chroniclers, a manuscript of the Pandects[30] preserved at Florence was venerated as a relic. People came on pilgrimage to see it, and two men, each holding a lighted candle in hand, stood, one to the right, the other to the left of the show-window where the much revered conjuring book received the homage of its devotees. This is sheer burlesque. A more serious phase of it is that from the eleventh century, the first law school in Europe, that of Bologna, propagated in the Occident the cult of *Corpus Juris Civilis* and refused thenceforth to recognize any other source of jurisprudence. The national law of the modern peoples was despised and derided by the jurists who prided themselves on their acquaintance with the masterpiece of Justinian, and thus it fell more and more into disuse. Meanwhile the Roman law began its triumphant course which was to end in the conquest of all Christendom. This infatuation for the Roman law may be explained partly by the incontestable superiority, which, under some aspects, it had over the Germanic law of the Middle Ages. The latter, born of ancient barbarian customs, preserved the stamp of the rudimentary society of which it was the expression. Written in crude language, it was almost exclusively penal and left unsolved most of the complex problems which result from the social relations of civilized men. It was devoid of all prestige in the eyes of the learned, it lacked the authority which comes from association with the name of a great jurist, it resembled one of these close fitting and curtailed garments which may suit a child but impede the gait of the adult. The Roman law, on the contrary, evolved during centuries by generations of learned men, appeared as a great monument, firm of foundation and indestructible in workmanship. It had the amplitude, the richness, the scientific precision worthy of a great civilization. In it all was foreseen, analyzed and judged by a luminous and profound intelligence which seemed to have penetrated the entire social life and which had acquired some sort of universality and infallibility. The Roman people, pre-eminently a juridical people, have produced nothing greater than the Roman law; and if one wishes to form an idea of the Roman people in the work which best represents their genius, one must study them in their legislative work. It is not astonishing, therefore, that the minds of men in the Middle Ages should have been dazzled at this aspect of the Roman law – much the same as the travellers of that period, who came from the northern cities before the erection of our great cathedrals, were wont to stop overawed at the sight of the Column of Trajan, the Coliseum, or the Baths of Caracalla. And as there is but a step from admiration to imitation, it is no wonder that the Middle Ages took the step and dreamed of making the *Corpus Juris Civilis* the code of the civilized world at that time.

## THE CHURCH AT THE TURNING POINTS OF HISTORY

*Roman law fosters unbridled absolutism or Caesarism.*

Here began the deplorable and tragic error. While from a scientific point of view, the Roman law was incontestably superior to the laws of the Middle Ages; while, with regard to civil relations, it displayed a perfection which the barbarian codes could not approach; on the other hand, from a political point of view, it enshrined a system from which, it seems, the minds of the free men of the Middle Ages should have turned away with horror. The most unbridled absolutism was proclaimed as a doctrine with unprecedented boldness and logic. According to the Roman law, the sovereign, that is, the emperor, was a veritable god. Not that the Roman skeptics and the unbelievers of the Empire imagined that he really possessed a divine nature – they knew the contrary but too well – but they conceded that he possessed over his subjects the same power that God Himself has over His creatures. The will of the emperor took the place of justice and law, or, to express it better, his will was law. And though that will was ordinarily but a cruel and depraved caprice, as in the case of such tyrants as Caligula,[31] Nero,[32] Domitian,[33] Commodus,[34] Caracalla,[35] Heliogabulus,[36] etc., the people bowed before it without resistance and without murmur, and from the depths of their agony greeted the master with the salutation of the dying gladiator. The pagan world could think of no other form of sovereign power, of no other manner of obeying it.

It is worth noting that the jurists of the Middle Ages, hypnotized by their *Corpus*, did not recoil before the monstrous theory of power so radically opposed to the Christian principles and to the Germanic traditions. Convinced of the ideal perfection of the Roman law, they did not see, or were not willing to see, that undeniable defect of the masterpiece. Apparently they regarded imperial absolutism, as the condition and the guarantee of the perfection of the Roman law. Doubtless they persuaded themselves that the authority of the sovereign should be unlimited in order to ensure the full enforcement of the law. Thus they accepted in its entirety the judicial inheritance of the Roman Empire; and Caesarism – which is the name given in history to the Roman theory of absolute power – became the first article of their political creed.

## THE CHURCH AND NEO-CAESARISM

Nor is it surprising that men born in a free society should become the apologists of absolutism and dream of bringing mankind back to slavery. Similar aberrations are not uncommon; the plea of system explains them without justifying them. Moreover, men very seldom perceive the consequences of the principles they admit; and many would shudder at the practical application of principles which they have advocated with the greatest ardor. This is a natural infirmity of the human mind, which it may be humiliating to admit, but which it would be puerile to deny.

### *Kings of Germany strive to apply Caesarism.*

When the jurists had sufficiently spread and developed their principles, there appeared sovereigns who were willing to apply them. They were the kings of Germany of the House of Swabia. The Hohenstaufen – a name derived from their paternal castle – had, moreover, great qualities of mind and, being possessed of boundless ambition, they became the ardent advocates of these doctrines whenever their thirst for power could profit by them. They were the first to put themselves forward as the legitimate and direct successors of the ancient Roman Emperors, in order that they might thus lay claim to all the power possessed by their assumed predecessors. Docile pupils of the jurists, they found in their teachings inspiration for their political conduct and they endeavored to put their maxims into practice.

But the world of the Middle Ages was not yet ripe for slavery. The Papacy protested, the communes arose in opposition, a portion of feudalism itself refused to exchange a suzerain for a master. Emperor Frederick Barbarossa, in striving to impose on Italy laws dictated by the unmitigated spirit of Caesarism, encountered the stubborn resistance of the Lombard cities. In 1176, he was conquered by these at the celebrated battle of Legnano and compelled to recognize solemnly the rights he had trampled underfoot. His grandson, Frederick II, renewed the attempt in the thirteenth century; but, defeated in turn and excommunicated by the Pope, he was completely overthrown, and died in time to escape witnessing the fall and extermination of his whole dynasty.

Thus, on two successive occasions, the jurists were the losers of the game. On two successive occasions the Catholic spirit triumphed over the theories of Caesarism; and, on the ruins of an empire which the emperors themselves had destroyed by their ambition, the Catholic spirit kept intact the great principle of the Christian republic of the Middle Ages. Europe remained a moral and religious unit under the international magistracy of peace entrusted to the Pope, who was the protector of right and the guardian of public liberties.

But, although in these two conflicts the nations had risen against the new idea, the idea was not dead:- battles do not kill ideas. The principles of Caesarism continued to spread among the jurists, and their number increased in a growing society which had more and more need of them. Thus simultaneously in all Europe there arose a caste of guiding minds who were imbued with a system of public law, anti-Christian in its essence, although often its adherents were themselves not conscious of its anti-Christian character. And the day came, half a century after their second defeat, when the jurists at last had their revenge.

*Philip the Fair struggles for absolutism against Boniface VIII.*

It was in France that they found their opportunity, and it was King Philip the Fair who gave it to them. Grandson of Louis IX, enjoying the prestige which the saintly king had reflected upon his crown and dynasty, himself one of the most tenacious and most imperious characters known in history, Philip the Fair had great power for either good or evil. But unfortunately he was surrounded by a group of jurists such as Enguerrand of Marigny, Peter Flotte, William of Plaisian, William of Nogaret, whose society formed in a way, his intellectual atmosphere. They imbued his mind with the new doctrine, and he emerged with the cold fanaticism of a despot, incapable of being stayed by a moral consideration and ready to sacrifice the whole universe to his ambition.

This man was to open a new phase of modern history:- indeed, his struggle against the Papacy is not merely an episode of the history of the Middle Ages, it is another turning point of universal history. Let us pause to consider the full importance of the struggle about to ensue.

## THE CHURCH AND NEO-CAESARISM

When Pope Boniface VIII ascended the Pontifical throne (1294), sad events desolated Christendom. St. John of Acre, the last city held by the Christians in the Holy Land, had just been re-conquered by the Muslims. Thus all Palestine had fallen into their hands, and the blood shed in its defense by two million Christians had flown in vain during two centuries! It was a bitter sorrow for the Papacy, and Boniface VIII, in donning what Dante calls the weight of the great mantle, felt the sorrow in all its bitterness. His dream was to remedy this terrible situation by re-establishing peace among all the Christian princes and by obtaining from them a new expedition to the Holy Land. To bring this about it was absolutely necessary to prevent the war which seemed imminent between the King of France, Philip the Fair, and the King of England, Edward the First. This wicked war threatened to kindle a conflagration throughout all Europe. The two opponents secured allies on all sides: Philip counted on Scotland, Edward on the Empire, on Flanders, on Brabant. But, at this moment, true to the duty of his office, the Pope intervened to recall to sentiments of humanity those furious fools who, under the most futile pretexts, were preparing to deluge the world with blood. He spoke to them in words at once noble, firm, affectionate and hopeful, such as one would expect from the Chief of Christendom. "Are these," he said in substance, "exploits worthy of you and of your ancestors, and is it in this way that you fulfil your obligations of hastening to the assistance of the Christians of the Holy Land?"[37] Giving in to the entreaties of the Pope and perhaps also to the voice of their Christian conscience, the two rivals agreed to sign a truce of one year, which was to expire on June 24, 1296. It was an achievement full of promise for the cause of civilization, and so the Pope must have judged it, for, on April 13, 1296, of his own authority, he renewed the truce for a period of two years, and declared it obligatory under pain of excommunication. However, in order to spare the self-love of the two kings and perhaps also because he had counted on their own spontaneous act, he had enjoined his legates to promulgate this truce only if the kings themselves did not take the initiative.[38]

Then was heard the voice of the King of France, striking, for the first time, a discordant note in the harmony of the social doctrine of the Middle Ages. Philip the Fair protested against the bull of the Pope; he refused even to listen to the reading of it before making the following declarations: "That the temporal government of his kingdom belonged to him alone; that in this matter he recognized no superior; that in this regard he would never submit to any living soul; that he wished to exercise his jurisdiction in his fiefs, defend his kingdom and pursue his right with the aid of his subjects, of his allies and of God; that the truce did not bind him. In matters spiritual, following the example of his predecessors, he was disposed to receive humbly the admonitions of the Holy See, like a true son of the Church."

He added that he accepted the mediation of the Pope, in the capacity of a private person and as a chosen arbiter, but in no way in the capacity of a recognized authority.

### *Declarations of Philip imply separation of politics and Christian morality.*

Bear in mind the declarations of Philip the Fair; they have a wide bearing and go far beyond the question which provoked them. To deny to the Pope the right of intervening between belligerent kings in order to impose peace upon them meant more than the weakening of the most glorious and the most beneficent prerogative of the Holy See, more than the destruction of the only obstacle which prevented ambitious criminals from upsetting the world and deluging it with blood. However disastrous from this point of view were the declarations of the King of France for the future of European civilization, they were still more baneful because of the principle which inspired them. For the first time since the beginning of Christianity, they proclaimed the separation of politics and morality. The contrary had been recognized up to that time, and the kings themselves had admitted that their governments should conform to the moral law of Christianity. Philip the Fair denied this implicitly, since he was not willing that the will of the sovereign should be bound in the name of the law. This was tantamount to declaring that the royal power knew no limit, and, as a matter of fact, it no longer would have any other limits than those of its own choosing. It is the pagan theory in all its nakedness: *the prince is above the law; his will is the law. As the king wills, so wills the law.* And during five centuries it continued to be the axiom that inspired all governments.

## THE CHURCH AND NEO-CAESARISM

It is well to note the origin of royal absolutism in Europe. We are at the antipodes of the Christian theory of power. The principles formulated by Philip the Fair were those which the Popes opposed and defeated in their twofold struggle against the Hohenstaufen; they were those which henceforth would be invoked whenever there was question of humiliating and belittling the Holy See, or whenever, despite the resistance of the Holy See, there was question of encroaching in one point or another upon the patrimony of Christian public right bequeathed the nations by former ages. And it is worthy of remark that a great number of historians, followed by a veritable mob of second-rate minds, persuade themselves with a naïveté almost ludicrous, that these theories of royal absolutism are Catholic theories. This is repeated to us every day in the polemics of the press, and I do not know what is more to be wondered at in the success of so bold a lie: the credulity of those who believe it or the audacity of those who circulate it.

### *Forbearance of Boniface VIII.*

How did Pope Boniface VIII treat the declaration of the King of France, which accentuated with unrestrained crudity the violent opposition of the new politics to Catholic tradition? They who know this Pontiff only through the traditional lies of the state historiography, have a ready answer: "He protested, he manifested his indignation, he hurled the thunders of excommunication upon the head of the bold king of France." Not at all! Boniface VIII took the insult, let pass without protest the sophistries of the new politics, consented even to accept arbitration under the humiliating conditions imposed by the King of France; namely, not in the capacity of an authority and in the quality of Sovereign Pontiff, but in the role of a private person and — these are the exact words – "as Benedict Cajetan."[39] Why such condescension and forbearance? Apparently because, for the Pope, all other considerations gave way to the interest of public peace, even those considerations which concerned the dignity of the Holy See itself. Indeed, the Holy See, with an abnegation and a zeal which never failed for a single instant, devoted itself whole and entire to the great task of reconciling France and England. Notice, for example, how the Holy See addressed the German Emperor Adolph of Nassau, one of the enemies of Philip the Fair, in order to prevent him from taking up arms:

"We have passed sleepless nights, assuming voluntarily the burden, in order to be able to establish peaceful relations between you and our sons in Christ, the illustrious kings, Philip of France and Edward of England, and to secure tranquillity to the Christian people, for the purpose of preventing the chiefs of the faithful and their subjects from turning against one another the swords which must be drawn in defense of the Holy Land and against the enemies of the Cross of Jesus Christ. And for this reason we warn you, we pray you, we exhort you earnestly and we entreat you, by the blood shed by Jesus Christ, not to attack the said King of France or his kingdom; but rather may your royal soul yield to our entreaties and be disposed to peace or at the very least to a long and sufficient truce, during which it will be possible to treat effectively of peace in our presence, through the envoys of the various parties."

At last, on June 27, 1298, Boniface VIII could render his sentence. It bore evidence of the purest equity, and certainly, as even French historians admit, it was not the King of France who had reason to complain. Indeed, the sentence approved the marriage of his daughter Isabella with the Prince of Wales, and through this union sacrificed the interests of the Count of Flanders, Guy of Dampierre, who had engaged in turn his two daughters to this prince and who saw them successively abandoned. But, as I have said already, in the eyes of the Pope, the cause of European peace led all other considerations. Finally, at the cost of many tribulations, he had obtained the result so ardently longed for, even though at the last moment the one who gained most from peace pretended that he hesitated to accept arbitration, as being too much to his disadvantage.

*Characteristics of first encounter between Pope and King.*

This was the first encounter between the Papacy and the new politics. I had to explain it in some detail, both because it is little known, and because it perfectly characterizes the attitudes of the two parties in the course of the long conflict which was about to open. The Papacy, as international magistracy and guardian of the general interests of

Christendom, undertook to safeguard peace between the nations, and in order to attain this great result, made all sacrifices and concessions compatible with its high dignity. The King of France had no such concern. His only preoccupation was to establish his absolutism in spite of the sovereign Pontiff as well as of his own subjects, and without any regard for the general welfare of civilization. What concerned the Pope was the peace of the world; what concerned the King was his unlimited power. We should add – for it is of importance – that in this struggle the Pope represented the Catholic tradition of Europe, the King the revolutionary aspirations of the jurists. We note this opposition, however evident, because the hired forgers have here reversed the roles. In their version it was the Pope who innovated and it was the King who defended himself.

### *Philip the Fair attacks immunities of the Church.*

The rest of the conflict between Boniface VIII and Philip the Fair presents the same characteristics as this first episode. The matter of ecclesiastical immunities, which broke out shortly afterwards, again brought in opposition the Papacy, which defended the traditional public right of Christian Europe, and the King, who sought to enthrone the revolutionary maxims of pagan rights. Philip was always in need of money, and his jurists had taught him that the possessions of his subjects belonged to him. Accordingly, he took whatever he could lay hands on. He took the possessions of the Knights Templars, he took the possessions of the Jews, he took the possessions of all the taxpayers by coining false money – it was natural that he should also wish to take the possessions of the Church.

But the possessions of the Church were protected by special immunities. In accordance with the doctrine of the time, they belonged to the poor and they could not be taxed. This did not mean, as some have asserted with inconceivable ignorance, that the Church did not contribute to the public expenses. Far from it! Only, it contributed in the form of voluntary donations, by giving over to the king, when he was in need of it, one tenth of its entire revenue. This was called the tithes. It has been calculated that in a little more than half a century, from 1247 to 1300, the French clergy paid to the king thirty-nine tithes, almost four times its entire revenue, or one-fifth of all its possessions. These figures attest that the exemption from taxation was for the Church a purely honorary privilege and that the patriotism of the clergy neutralized its immunities. Their *voluntary donations* were more burdensome than an obligatory tax would have been.

When, in 1295, the clergy were asked to pay a new tithe, they protested and, upon repeated and persistent demands, appealed to the Pope. The Pope was the guardian of the privileges of the entire Church and the protector of all her rights; when called upon by the clergy of France, he was strictly bound, under pain of failing in his most sacred obligations, to come to the rescue of the oppressed, and he did. I shall not relate the varying fortunes of this new conflict with the crown. It will suffice to state that here again the Pope showed the greatest forbearance towards the prevaricating King. The Pope recalled to the mind of the King, as was his duty, that he had no right to impose taxes upon the clergy without the consent of the Pope, but he assured the King that he would never refuse his consent whenever there would be question of the defense of the kingdom and that he would sell the sacred treasures rather than endanger so great a cause. He added that in case of urgent and very evident necessity, he would even permit that they should proceed without awaiting his consent, but that, in all other cases, they should submit to the law. One must admit that this was pushing the spirit of conciliation as far as justice permitted, and, thanks to the moderation of both, the conflict was once more avoided.

*Philip attacks Pope's ambassador.*

But peace was to be short-lived. Contempt of law was always the characteristic trait of Philip the Fair; he did not seem to enjoy the fullness of the royal prerogative so long as he encountered any limits to his power. One day the Pope sent a messenger to ask for the release of the unfortunate Count of Flanders, Guy of Dampierre, who was languishing in the prisons of the king. The ambassador, who was entrusted with a message so worthy of the Father of the faithful, was Bernard Saisset, Bishop of Pamiers. What took place in the interview between the

King and the Bishop? We do not know, but the King pretended that the ambassador had used language that was not respectful, and he pursued the unfortunate prelate with incredible rancor. He demanded that the Pope should take from him his episcopal charter and even the privilege of clerical immunity,[40] in order that he himself might afterwards impeach him before a lay tribunal and have him condemned as a state criminal. This demand was a veritable mockery. One might say that the King was jesting in exacting of the Pope, at one and the same time, the violation of all the most sacred rights: the respect due to a bishop, the lawful immunity of the priest, the sacred character of the ambassador, not to speak of the ignominy in imposing upon the Pope such odious measures against his legate whose only crime was that he had served his master!

The Pope replied with calm dignity and fortitude; he called up the cause of Bernard Saisset at his own tribunal, and he took steps to convene a council in Rome to adopt measures to meet the situation. At the same time he addressed the tyrant himself in the bull *Ausculta fili*, where he set forth his grievances. The tone of the document is disclosed by its very title (*Listen, my son*). To these legitimate measures, the King prompted by his jurists, replied with unheard of violence and deceit. He convened the States-General of France, had read to them a false papal bull which had been made up by his men-of-law, in which they put haughty and scornful language into the mouth of the Sovereign Pontiff, ordered a jurist to read a reply to the Pope which was a tissue of revolting calumnies, and, as a result of these infamous maneuvers, he obtained from the deceived and terrorized States-General a bill of indemnity for his conduct towards the Pope.

*Philip causes arrest of Pope.*

This time the cup of patience was full to overflowing. The Pope fulminated the bull *Unam Sanctam*, a solemn and moderate exposition of the pure Catholic doctrine on the relations between the two powers, in accordance with the tradition of the Church, such as might have been formulated by Gregory VII, Alexander III[41] or Innocent III.[42] At the time, he prepared the excommunication of the prevaricating King. Then Philip the Fair decided to make his final stroke. Surpassing all his past crimes, he dispatched to Italy one of the vilest insulters of the Pope, William of Nogaret, with the mission to instigate a plot against the Holy See. The wretch, after having endeavored to shake the fidelity of the Roman people, set out for Anagni with the intention of surprising the old man in his little town. Boniface was without defense. He donned his pontifical insignia, and, holding in his hand the keys of St. Peter, awaited his enemies. Neither this grandeur of soul, nor the majesty of the Vicar of Jesus Christ, nor the white hair of a man of eighty-six years, moved the criminals. The Pope remained in their power for three days; the third day the inhabitants of Anagni rose in opposition and drove them out. Boniface did not wish that they should be pursued, but so many emotions had broken his strength and a few days afterwards he expired.

Great was the indignation of the Christian world on hearing of the attempt made at Anagni. Dante, despite his supposed grievance against the venerable Pope, has forever branded the contemptible authors of the dastardly assault in these immortal verses: "I see the *fleurs de lis* enter Anagni, I see the Christ imprisoned in His Vicar, I see Him again given over to derision, I see Him again drenched with vinegar and gall, and crucified between new thieves."[43]

*Philip attacks memory of Boniface.*

This judgment of the greatest poet of the Middle Ages is also the honest judgment of humanity, and the cowardly courtiers of royal absolutism were not unaware of it; accordingly, following the example of the royal malefactor, they worked with boundless fury and cynicism to pervert the opinion of posterity. After having outraged their victim, they wished to disgrace him; after having grieved him to death, they attempted to dishonor his name. It would be difficult to form an idea of the intense rancor with which Philip the Fair strove to bring into contempt the memory of Boniface VIII with his successors: he was foiled in his attempt, but the diversion was cleverly made to turn attention away from his own crimes and, in this at least, he succeeded. As to the official historiographers, especially such as Dupuy, Baillet and others, they continued the tradition bequeathed them by the jurists of Philip

## THE CHURCH AND NEO-CAESARISM

the Fair. They fabricated some documents; they falsified others; when they could neither destroy nor alter, they at least changed the dates, to modify their bearing and often to make them express a contrary meaning; in a word, they have heaped upon the memory of Boniface VIII such a load of lies and calumnies, that after five centuries we have not yet succeeded in clearing entirely the field of history.

### *Modern French historians exonerate Boniface.*

Nevertheless the hour of justice has struck. Now that royal absolutism, defeated in turn, no longer has at its service the corrupt pens of its flatterers, the French historians themselves today admit to what extent their kings made travesty of truth at a time when it was to their profit to disfigure it. They admit, too, that, in this resounding drama, the aggression came not from the Papacy, which was content with defending its traditional position, but from the royal power, which, armed with the theories of Caesarism, sought the overthrow of a political regime which was based on the religious unity of the world and on the indirect power of the Sovereign Pontiffs. "Boniface VIII," writes Mr. Boutaric in a celebrated book, "did not bring new pretensions to the See of Peter: his politics towards outside princes were those of his predecessors."[44] But no one will contend that the politics of Philip the Fair were those of St. Louis: they were, at the most, those of Frederick of Swabia, and these, in last analysis, were the politics of the Roman Caesars. In other words, they were pagan politics, making a fresh effort to take the guidance of these modern states away from Christian principles.

I have already stated that these politics have triumphed and I have indicated, in the beginning of this lecture, what connivances they found at an early hour in the social body. In conclusion I wish to indicate briefly the results of their victory.

### *Evil results of neo-Caesarism.*

It was, first of all, the destruction of what has been called the Christian Republic of the Middle Ages. Up to then Europe was strongly united not only by the identity of religious beliefs but also by the identity of political maxims. It connected public right with Christian morality, and recognized as the interpreter of the latter the Vicar of Jesus Christ. From the time of Philip the Fair it was so no more. There was no longer a Christian Republic, as was evidenced by the disappearance of what was its wonderful manifestation – the Crusades. St. Louis had been the last of the Christian kings, he was also the last of the Crusaders. And Europe, which up to that time had carried the standard of the Cross to Jerusalem, to Tunis, to Damascus, recoiled before the Crescent. They had to give back Jerusalem and hand over Constantinople to Islam. Mohammed became again the arbiter of the Mediterranean and the Turks the terror of the world. We can blame neo-Caesarism for plunging the most beautiful lands of the earth into barbarism. Behold, from an international point of view, the balance sheet of royal absolutism!

From a national point of view the absolutism of kings has broken the equilibrium of the social body, concentrated all the life in the head, atrophied free institutions and made revolution the only possible corrective of tyranny. Nor is that all. The Christian nations wrenched from the guidance of the Church have not found their way; they seem condemned to travel the whole cycle of error before finding their way again. Ever and anon they turn to new systems which become bankrupt one after another. Philosophism, liberalism, socialism, anarchism, to say nothing of the intermediate doctrines, are the legitimate heirs of royal absolutism; like it, they will betray their promises. The unrest will last as long as the destiny of the Christian nations remains in the hands of a political system which does not worry about Christian principles. The Catholic Church, seated at the foot of the Cross, waits calmly for the day when revolution shall have finished the education of mankind.[45]

Chapter VI

# THE CHURCH AND THE RENAISSANCE

*The Renaissance is a natural development of society of Middle Ages.*

THE RENAISSANCE IS, UNQUESTIONABLY, ONE OF THE most remarkable phenomena in the history of humanity. At the outset it is well to note that the term *Renaissance* or *Revival of learning* is a misnomer for the vast intellectual movement of the fifteenth and sixteenth centuries. What really took place was not so much a revival of learning as a flowering out of the learning of preceding centuries. It is a capital error to hold that this epoch marks an abrupt and sudden resurrection of intellectual life after long centuries of darkness. In history, as in nature, there can be no effect without a cause. From nothing comes nothing; all are bound together by the law of cause and effect. The movement of the Renaissance was in keeping with the laws of accelerated motion: it was but the natural, progressive and uninterrupted development of the society of the Middle Ages from century to century down to the opening of the present age. Modern genius had for parent the society of the Middle Ages and grew up with it during the laborious and fruitful centuries of its infancy; finally, it reached the heyday of youth when, like an opening flower, it disclosed suddenly all its rich and magnificent vitality.

This view of the Renaissance is in keeping with all the laws of nature and all the teachings of history. As Pascal, the well-known French philosopher, remarks, "The whole succession of men should be considered as one man who lives on and never ceases to learn." This is especially true of modern society. From the days of Charlemagne down to the sixteenth century, modern society had not ceased to develop its acquired knowledge and increase its intellectual capital. On a certain day it found itself rich without being able to mark the precise moment when its poverty had changed into wealth. Nothing would be more interesting than to study the different phases of this intellectual progress as they succeeded one another in the course of the ages, such as the revival under Charlemagne – the development of modern languages – the progress of these languages alongside of the scientific language – the birth of popular poetry and the great epics – the appearance of the poetry of love and chivalry – the troubadours and the *minnesingers* – the theater with its original setting – the great philosophical and theological discussions of the twelfth century – the advent of experimental science with Roger Bacon[46] – the vast intellectual movement created by the powerful impulse of the Crusades – the elaboration of the encyclopaedias in which such geniuses as Thomas of Aquin, Albert the Great,[47] and such compilers as Vincent of Beauvais[48] summarized the knowledge of their times – the splendor of the plastic arts which covered all Europe with unequaled monuments – the great voyages of exploration which, from the beginning of the sixteenth century, opened up a new and strange horizon by advancing beyond the circle of existing knowledge – and then the inventions which hastened the march of progress and made new advances possible to mankind.

A few examples will illustrate my meaning. The fact that Christopher Columbus discovered the West Indies and Vasco da Gama the East Indies does not signify that these two explorers were wonderful initiators who, appearing like meteors, drew humanity after them into fields hitherto unexplored. No! They were the heirs of those intrepid Portuguese navigators who, in a series of voyages that had extended over more than a century, had explored the entire coast of Western Africa as far as the mouth of the Congo, leaving to their successors the task of finishing the work and appropriating all the glory. In like manner when Gutenberg discovered the art of multiplying the works which contained the best that human genius had produced, he was but applying in an ingenious manner the ideas of the monks who, many centuries before, consecrated their lives to copying manuscripts, "piercing the devil with as many strokes as they traced characters upon paper." Gutenberg was the immediate successor – the intellectual heir – of those *Brothers of the pen* who had thought out the solution of the same problem by making themselves, so to speak, living writing-machines.

It would be easy to continue this review, for everywhere we cannot but notice that existing capital is always abundantly productive and that, at a given moment, there results inevitably an enormous increase of social wealth. This intellectual phenomenon of the sixteenth century is similar to the economic phenomenon witnessed at the beginning of the nineteenth century, when machinery multiplied production indefinitely and threw upon the markets, for the use of all, an incalculable quantity of industrial products. Just as the discovery of machinery was made possible only by reason of the vast conquests of the natural sciences, dating from the sixteenth century, so in like manner the conquests of the sixteenth century were prepared and worked out by the sustained and constant efforts of the generations of the Middle Ages. The intellectual life of the world at that time may be likened to the top of a ladder, each rung of which was occupied by a generation. The luscious fruits which ripen on the tree of civilization are the last results of an innumerable series of patient and disinterested efforts; they represent the succession of generations that have disappeared.

Such being the true view of the Renaissance, it is amusing to read the contention of many writers that this imposing phenomenon was due to the fact that Greek professors, driven from the Orient by the Turkish invasions, happened to bring to amazed Western Europe the literary treasures of antiquity. These treasures of antiquity were in possession of Western Europe before the coming of the professors; from the professors it took but a small part of these treasures at a time when, by its own efforts, it had become capable of appreciating them. The revival of ancient literature in Western Europe is a consequence, not the origin, of the Renaissance.

*The Renaissance leads some to imitate morals of pagan antiquity.*

But all wealth – material or intellectual – has its dangers. Material riches enervate the heart by voluptuousness, intellectual riches puff up the mind with pride. And when the Gospel says: "Woe to the rich!," we may believe that these hard words apply not only to those who bend under the load of gold but also to those who succumb beneath the weight of knowledge. Neither the one nor the other can enter the Kingdom of God, if they are not poor in spirit, that is, if they do not use their treasures for the higher ends of charity. And I am convinced that it was especially to those who have attained the heights of intellectual life that the Lord wished to teach a lesson when He placed a child in the midst of His disciples and declared that heaven is closed to those who are not like unto that little one.

Now, it was to this danger, inherent in all riches and which consists in loving riches for themselves, that many men of this epoch succumbed. I do not speak of those who became attached to material wealth and to the sensual enjoyments it procures; the voluptuaries do not count in history, their social action is null, they represent the purely negative element in the destinies of humanity. Here we are concerned with those who, in modern parlance, are called the *intellectuals* – those who assimilated all the culture of their times and reacted on the minds of their contemporaries. For many of these intellectual life had the effect of an intoxicant: it inebriated them. They knew no measure in their enjoyment. They refused to heed the moral law of moderation. They would be humanists above all else, they were not much concerned about remaining Christians. Like the jurists of the twelfth century they gave themselves body and soul to the worship of antiquity. They were pagans because the ancients were pagans and, according to the energetic expression of Holy Writ, they became like to their idol.

Does this mean that one may not study antiquity without succumbing to its spell, without becoming pagan in mind and heart? Far from it! We have instances to the contrary. The Carolingian revival remained thoroughly Christian in inspiration, notwithstanding the preponderant part it gave to ancient literature; and the powerful geniuses of the thirteenth century, although mainly nourished by antiquity, borrowed from it only its beneficent elements and remained conscious of their own superiority. St. Thomas of Aquin has not enslaved modern thought to the philosophy of his master Aristotle; rather, he made Aristotle contribute to the demonstration of Christian truth. Dante Alighieri was devoted to Virgil and saw in him the personification of human knowledge, but he surpassed Virgil in that he loved Beatrice, the symbol of divine knowledge. These are illustrious models from whom the men of the fifteenth and sixteenth centuries might have drawn inspiration. In fact, there were a great number among the humanists of that time whom literature did not turn from Christianity; among others were Rudolph Agricola,[49] Vittorina da Feltre, Aleandro,[50] Maffeo Vegio, Sadoleto,[51] Vida,[52] Pico della Mirandola,[53] Alexander Hegius,[54] Thomas More,[55] Cardinal Fisher,[56] Louis Vives,[57] our own admirable Cleynaerts.[58]

But we must admit that all minds have not the same degree of virtue or of intellectual health. Many fell victims to the poisonous perfume which issued from the tomb of antiquity. They were not startled by the vices which Christian morality reproves, when these vices were idealized and surrounded with all the prestige of poetry. They envied the absolute liberty of ancient thought which, free from the fetters of truth, wandered at will in the boundless field of philosophic speculation. Often, unwittingly, they were drawn away from the sure positions which Christian education had secured for mind and heart. They lowered the water-mark of morality to bring it down to the level of antiquity; they let go the truths which they thought enchained them but which in reality sustained them.

The result was inevitable. The hope that they might keep themselves intact with imaginations so infatuated was as vain as the pretensions of certain young men of our time who, under pretext of literary studies, ask of their confessor permission to read all the productions of the pornographic writers of our day, believing that they can escape from such association with unsullied imagination, sound moral judgment, unswerving will! Thus the passionate study of the Greeks and Romans produced on the different classes of admirers various phenomena. We shall classify these phenomena and then strive to estimate them at their true value.

*The Renaissance leads all
to exaggerate literary merits of pagan antiquity.*

In the sixteenth century everyone – the best Christians as well as the most pronounced pagans – fell with exemplary docility under the literary charm of antiquity. We may call this the *minimum* of pagan influence. It was the universal conviction that the ancients had conceived types of the beautiful which could never be equalled, and that we moderns have to imitate these types unvaryingly, if we wish in turn to realize an aesthetic ideal. No one doubted that the ancients had created the moulds into which we must cast the productions of our own genius if we would escape the penalty of producing barbarous and monstrous works; and that our highest artistic effort was to imitate the ancients and thus to reach the perfection of the works which they had drawn from their imagination. It was irrevocably decreed that the role of creator was reserved to antiquity and that the modern age must content itself with the character of imitator.

This odd conception of aesthetic life is explained in great measure by the ignorance of those who formulated it. For a long time past the Middle Ages had ceased to be known, nor were they to be known again for a long time to come. The judgments of Boileau, in his *Art Poétique*, are very significant in this respect. He was convinced – and he expresses his conviction with delightful assurance – that our devout forefathers knew no kind of poetry, were ignorant of rhythm, and were without the pleasures of the theatre. These assertions will appear absurd to him who knows that the troubadours[59] and the *minnesingers*[60] of the Middle Ages are the fathers of modern lyric poetry, that from that period date all our epics – the incomparable *Chanson de Roland*,[61] the *Poem of the Cid*,[62] the *Nibelungenlied*,[63] the *Roman de Renard*,[64] – that the theatre never enjoyed greater popularity nor exerted a greater social influence than in the Middle Ages. No wonder that in our own day Littré lectures good Nicholas Despréaux Boileau and suggests that his judgments are hardly worthy of the author of the *Art Poétique*.

But there is something more than ignorance in the literary view of the people of the sixteenth and seventeenth centuries: there is a real infatuation. It was, alas, at that time that good Father Maffei sought permission to read his Breviary in Greek, that his style might not be spoiled by the bad Latin of the Church. It was at that time that Ferreri, who had been entrusted by Leo X with the reform of the Latin Breviary, disfigured its most beautiful hymns under pretext of removing its barbarisms, treated the Blessed Virgin as a nymph and a goddess, and spoke of God as the sovereign of the gods. And what are we to say of the prejudices regarding plastic art! Men who lived and died under the shadow of our marvellous Gothic cathedrals disfigured these noble monuments to make them look like the Greek temples with their feeble and cold beauty. They had under their eyes the radiant majesty of the portals of Rheims, of Paris and of Amiens – and they despised them! One of the most enlightened and, certainly, one of the most sympathetic of the great writers of the seventeenth century – our good Fénelon – formulated against the art of our fathers a condemnation whose every line and whose every word is an outrage against truth, good taste and aesthetic sense. This strange blindness can find explanation only in the *a priori* conviction that there is no beauty except in ancient art and in its imitations: the absolute artistic superiority of the ancients was an axiom as incontestable as the dogmas of the Christian faith.

*Infatuation with pagan antiquity
begets in some contempt for Christianity.*

In vain would one have tried to make these persons understand that they were injuring Christianity in considering it incapable of attaining an ideal of beauty; they would have replied to you with Boileau:

De la religion les mystères terribles
D'ornements égayés ne sont pas susceptibles.[65]

And if one had urged the matter further, they would have declared that there is nothing in common between religion and aesthetics – very much as in our own day, in our own country (Belgium), some members of the Right say there is nothing in common between religion and economic questions, while members of the Left say that there is nothing in common between religion and politics.

Who does not see that already there was, even among the best, a real diminution of the Christian faith, since they excluded its influence from the whole vast intellectual domain, dividing their minds into two compartments – one reserved to art and poetry, the other to religion. They did not know, or they had lost sight of the fact, that Christianity is like the sun which must penetrate everything to vivify everything; that there is such a thing as Christian aesthetics just as there is Christian politics and Christian economics; that the beautiful, like the true and the good, is one of the aspects of the Supreme Being, God; and that, in art as in nature, nothing is beautiful which does not bear on its brow the reflection of the uncreated Beauty. It seems that in those days no one suspected these truths which are an integral part of Christian doctrine; they had to await the *Genius of Christianity* by Châteaubriand to be reminded of the fact that the Catholic religion possesses some beauty.

Imbued with such veneration for ancient literature, how could one keep himself free from a like infatuation for the civilization of which this literature was the expression? For the genius of ancient literature with seductive eloquence and poetic beauty depicted the ancient world in a radiant and almost divine light. And the men of the Renaissance, viewing it through a halo, pictured to themselves an antiquity which had never existed, an antiquity where everything was beautiful and grand, luminous and serene, where nobility of heart went side by side with largeness of mind, an antiquity where all things human took on more than natural proportions, where the historic heroes had the gait of demi-gods, and from which emerged sages, walking with their disciples in the shade of the Grove of Academus,[66] discussing the existence of God and the immortality of the soul. Thus the Christian imagination of the men of the Renaissance projected its own mental image on the clouds which veiled the past and, without knowing it, admired itself in a world which was nothing but its own reflection.

But it may be objected that there is no great harm in all this and that we have here but one of those ever recurring illusions which will never cease to baffle men. But this contention will hardly hold, for I notice that all who have professed this enthusiastic veneration for the ancients have been correspondingly unjust towards Christian society and Christianity. If it were true that the most noble representatives of the human race are found among the pagans, if it were true, as Thiers[67] stated in an official report, "that antiquity is the most beautiful thing in the world," then, to be logical, one would have to say with the poet:

No need there were for Mary to give birth.[68]

In other words Christianity would be useless – nay more – it would be responsible for the decadence of humanity, if since its advent mankind had lost all that constitutes true genius. Christianity would have been but an empty parenthesis: by closing the parenthesis and returning to the sources of antiquity, the human mind would find itself again and resume the interrupted course of its glorious destinies.

# THE CHURCH AND THE RENAISSANCE

*Some admirers of the Renaissance
attempt to paganize the modern world.*

This conclusion was so logical that it soon found some who had the courage to deduce it. In contradistinction of those naïve persons who Christianized antiquity, they would paganize the modern world – and they began the experiment with themselves. They took from antiquity its manner of thinking and its way of living. Shaking from their minds the yoke of dogma and from their hearts the burden of the moral law, they undertook to use, as they liked, the powerful faculties of thinking and of willing which belong to man and whose use providential laws have at all times regulated. They wantonly stripped themselves of the twofold superiority which they owed to Christianity, and rejoiced in descending again to the level of pagan naturalism, where grace was absent. They forgot the origin of man, they forgot, above all, his last end; they abandoned that narrow road by which the Master wished us to enter into eternal life; they took the broad way of living, which knows neither the joys of sacrifice freely accepted, nor the consolations of sorrow borne with resignation, nor the sublime delights of charity which raises man up to God. For them, as for the ancients, their whole existence was centered on voluptuousness and glory – this was their twofold ideal of life.

Of voluptuousness I shall not speak, except to state that no ancient was exempt from its defilements, that the most celebrated men of antiquity, even when they triumphed over their senses, mastered them for the time only, to succumb to them later. There did not exist among the pagans a soul truly proof against voluptuousness, and, if one were found, the exception would but prove the rule.

Love of glory is no doubt a more elevated sentiment, and at times we find in antiquity examples of it which command our respect. I know of no more beautiful instance of it than the words spoken by the dying Epaminondas in reply to those who lamented that he left no children to inherit his glory: "Friends, I die content; I leave two immortal daughters, Leuctra and Mantinea."[69] Noble and proud words and worthy of a hero! Nevertheless there are other words more beautiful. "Da mihi nesciri!" (Grant me, O Lord, to remain unknown!) Thus spoke the author of the most beautiful book ever penned by the hand of man – we do not here consider the inspired Gospel – and this wish of the sublime author of the

Imitation has been realized for five centuries: he has remained hidden behind his masterpiece, greater in his effacement than the Theban in the exaltation of his name.[70] One should not despise the love of glory when it becomes a stimulant to great actions, but we must admit that Christian humility has been productive of greater actions and of actions which cost less to society. To reverse the role of these two motives and to exalt the former at the expense of the latter would be a step backward in civilization.

It would have been less objectionable if, in reviving the passion of antiquity for the perpetuation of one's name, the humanists of the Renaissance had at least followed the noble idea of Epaminondas and not the manner of the pedants. For most of them were pedants indeed, dreaming that immortality might come to them from a well-turned distich, or a new expression, or a pleasant saying. Read in the *Femmes Savantes* of Molière the scene between Trissotin and Vadius, and you will have acquaintance with almost all the pagan and semi-pagan humanists of the Renaissance. In their books, in their correspondence, in their conversation, there is in evidence a childish vanity, an extreme susceptibility, an amazing infatuation. If you but seem to touch with disrespectful hands one of the rays of their halo, at once these demi-gods will turn against you in coarse invectives, hurl at your head all the abuse of the fish woman's vocabulary, forgetting that, though immortals, they are talking and acting as street porters! This is all the more pitiful when one considers that, with all their pretensions to renown, most of these great men have drawn on posterity letters of exchange which posterity has allowed to be protested. Erasmus of Rotterdam, our quasi-compatriot, is the most celebrated and the most estimable type of this class of minds. In his own time he was adulated as a god and actually looked upon himself as a guiding genius, whilst he was simply a bookman crammed with Latin and Greek, although we must admit that he had well digested these languages.

If from the thinkers we pass on to the men of action, we shall find paganism put into practice with astounding boldness. At this time we find a legion of men who had entirely given up the Christian idea that they might conform to the pagan morality of pleasure and success. They abounded in all ranks of society, were not lacking among the clergy, and, alas, were to be found even on the Chair of Peter. Pope Alexander VI is the most sinister incarnation of paganism under the tiara: serene and smiling amidst the mire of vices, he displayed with an astonishing lack of conscience the spectacle of his turpitudes; and even in the winter of old age, he prolonged, beneath the eyes of an astonished world, the wild revel of an existence lacking in moral sense.

Alexander VI is the type of the voluptuary – nothing more.[71] His son Caesar Borgia presents to us the most finished type of the pagan politician. Young, beautiful, brave, intelligent, friend of the arts, model of courtesy, he is, in spite of all these external qualities, the most cruel, the most perverse, the most unscrupulous of men. The conquest of the greatest possible power and glory is for him the only ideal of life, and it seems never to have entered his mind that such an ideal could be limited by any moral law. "There is nothing in common between religion and politics! Politics is an art which one cultivates for itself and which knows but one law, that of success." Thus Caesar Borgia was taught by his master, the most genial, the most atrocious of all the representatives of the Renaissance, the man whose name has been given to a political system of deceit and immorality, a system which utterly ignores Christianity:- this man is Nicholas Machiavelli.

Strikingly expressive is the portrait of this heartless and unfeeling genius, which may be seen today in the Uffizi Gallery at Florence. Note the excessively sharp profile, the cruel fox-like snout, where you may read the combination of sanguinary baseness of instinct and wonderful acumen of mind: you will catch yourself shivering, and you will quickly turn away with an impression of uneasiness and fright. Moreover Machiavelli has left us a portrait of himself in his writings, especially in his treatise *The Prince* which for centuries has been the breviary of absolute monarchs, even of those who wrote anti-Machiavellian books, as Frederick II of Prussia.[72] It is not necessary to state that Machiavelli had no more morals than faith, and that this almost diabolical contemnor of the Papacy led a private life which was but a tissue of infamies.

I have mentioned only a few characteristic types; but in order to make known all the varieties of pagan celebrities of this epoch, it would be necessary to give other names beginning with Lorenzo della Valle, who boldly professed in his writings the principles of the most abject epicurism, down to Pomponazzi, who did not fear to deny the doctrine of the immortality of the soul and who ended his life by suicide. To give an idea of the moral and intellectual atmosphere of the time, one should at least recall the extraordinary fortune of the ignoble Aretino, a sort of Leo Taxil of the sixteenth century, though possessing more talent, before whom princes trembled, and who touched the pocket-books of kings who feared the power of this pamphleteer. All these persons, by their talent, by their boldness, by their number, and through skilful grouping, give the impression that they are the true representatives of their time, the general expression of the spirit of the Renaissance. And, indeed, if the intellectual movement which bears this name must be judged by the men who took control of it, it is certain that the Renaissance was a return to the ideas and the aspirations of paganism. We deny this conclusion because we reject the premises – but it was very easy to be deceived therein.

*Some condemned whole movement because of its abuses.*

People were deceived from the first. Many sincere minds were alarmed at the unheard of licentiousness of thought, often followed by a like licentiousness of morals, and they attributed to the intellectual movement itself the scandals which were but an abuse. They decried art, literature and science, because they held these to be directly responsible for the moral and religious crisis of their time. Seeing that intellectual culture produced such fruits, they turned from it and confined themselves to divine science. This is, alas, today as then, the conduct honest people who have more good will than keenness of mind, in whom are verified the words of the Gospel that the children of darkness are wiser in their generation than the children of light. The temptation to act thus is so strong that, for the greater number, it is well-nigh irresistible. It is so expeditious, so convenient, for minds of narrow vision, to condemn as a whole all intellectual and social progress because of the abuses to which it gives occasion!

This narrowness of view, though it usually shelters itself under the cloak of religion, really injures religion by making it appear opposed to all progress and incompatible with every development of civilization. This is not the broad and vivifying spirit of Christianity, it is the narrow-mindedness of the grossest fanaticism which dictates, at all epochs, the attitude of reactionaries. "If these books say the same things as the

Koran, they are useless; if they say the contrary, they are hurtful; in either case, they must be burned." This language is worthy of Calif Omar setting fire to the library of Alexandria; but it is too often held by zealous Christians, without suspecting that they are such good Muslims! It was, for instance, in 1507, the language of Adrian de Corneto, who using other words of comparison, strove to establish that all science is contained in Holy Writ and that it is folly to seek it elsewhere.

It was likewise the language of the rigorists of the moral order, who correctly attributed the corruption of their time to luxury, and who imagined that they could remedy it by bringing back the people, if need be by force, to the simplicity of morals and to the observance of the evangelical counsels. They dreamed of changing the world into a vast convent where each inhabitant would be subject to the severe observance of monastic rules, and where in a gigantic *auto-da-fé* they would burn, today all the products of frivolous and corrupting luxury, tomorrow all those who would not foreswear its worship. What a beautiful dream for high and visionary minds, who thought they could do without human liberty in the establishment of the Kingdom of God! So they often dreamed in those republics partly democratic, partly theocratic, such as the Puritans founded in the American colonies, and Calvin[73] in the Commune of Geneva. We recognize the same character in the enterprise of that high-minded enthusiast, the monk Jerome Savonarola, whose noble ideals and sincere zeal for the Catholic faith are beyond question. This unfortunate reformer was dictator of Florence long enough to get the notion that he had realized his ideal and also to draw upon himself the furious opposition which brought him to the funeral pyre.

Savonarola did not understand the law of growth which rules mankind, as it rules nature, and which does not permit society – any more than the individual – to have the same manners and the same mode of life in its old age as in its early years. Like the individual, humanity passes through various phases and while it always retains its elemental character it presents a diversity in its manifestations. Gradually, as it advances, it strips itself of the traits of youth to put on those of old age; it loses buoyancy to gain experience; it gathers the fruits of its former labors, extends its knowledge, sweetens the relations among men, studies itself and calls to its activities the control of the moralist and of the scientist. In thus developing itself according to its nature, society does not put itself in contradiction to Christianity, because the faith of Jesus Christ does not condemn any human faculty nor demand of civilization the sacrifice of any of its conquests, provided these labors and all the enjoyments which flow from them remain subordinate to the higher law of charity. When then, righteously moved by the miseries of his time, Savonarola thought to remedy them by reforms which offended nature and which were worse than the evil itself, he acted blindly and was bound to provoke the frightful reaction of which he himself was the first and most pathetic victim.

### *The Catholic Church on the contrary headed the movement in the right direction.*

The Catholic Church did not enter the way into which Savonarola wished to draw her. In the face of the great movement of the Renaissance, she remembered her eternal mission; she recalled not only that she is the religion of people still in infancy and of poor communities, but also that she is to lead to God the rich nations and enlightened civilization. Far from cursing the riches of science and the opulence of arts – though she often saw them misused – she blessed them and wished to make them contribute to the glory of God and the salvation of souls. And, with this largeness of view and this boldness of enterprise which we have recognized in her in former crises, instead of opposing the future and being crushed by it, instead of holding aloof and being left behind, she boldly grasped the banner of intellectual progress and headed the movement which drew humanity towards its mighty destinies.

I do not say that this attitude of the Church towards the Renaissance was always the result of formal deliberation, or that the chiefs of the hierarchy were always conscious of the fateful bearing of the part they played. Were they themselves, as private persons, not subject to the charm of artistic and literary life; and does not their surrender to the seductions that surrounded them sufficiently explain the interest of the Church in art and literature? And were there not among them some who became intoxicated with the wine of the Renaissance to the point of totally forgetting the Catholic spirit, forgetting that they were priests, bishops, cardinals, remembering only that they were humanists? But it is precisely because the movement was of such intensity that one is astonished that, instead of allowing herself to be drawn on by the current, the Church should have undertaken to direct it and that she should have succeeded in a large measure. She did not cry anathema against it, as the busy-bodies would have wished; she did not sacrifice the legitimate demands of the Christian spirit, as did the humanists; she proposed to create, in the full meaning of the term, a revival which would be Catholic – and she succeeded. The names of Pius II, Nicholas V, Julius II, and Leo X recall the most powerful and the most efficacious protection which the intellectual life of the human race ever received from a sovereign authority.

I do not intend here to recount in detail the history of this incomparable patronage of science, art and literature, or to show the Sovereign Pontiffs surrounded by the glorious phalanx of artists – at their head the unrivaled Bramante,[74] Michelangelo[75] and the divine Raphael.[76] But I may say in general and without fear of exaggeration that no century has seen – that probably no century will ever see – such an ensemble of works as the Dome of St. Peter's, the Sistine Chapel, the Stanze and the Loggie of the Vatican. If – unlike Jerusalem, Antioch, Athens, Baghdad, and Cordova – Rome is not today a tomb in ruins, with her grandeur forever destroyed; if the Eternal City is ever resplendent, in the eyes of the entire world, with the incomparable splendor which surrounds her sanctuaries, her museums, her libraries; if the world does not cease to go to her in pilgrimage as to the living center of civilization, it is to the Popes of the Renaissance that she is indebted. It is not the ruins of some monuments of antiquity which would entitle her, in the eyes of the world, so far to outrank Athens with its Parthenon, or Treves with its *Porta Nigra*. The Popes have made the Eternal City a page of apologetics, written under their dictation by the greatest artists of the world, a page which will speak from century to century with superhuman eloquence.

But here, as in all other things, Rome is but the symbol of the Catholic Church herself. Thanks to the Popes of the Renaissance, the Catholic Church wears henceforth upon her brow a new tiara, which renders her sacred even in the eyes of those who despise the Renaissance: it is the threefold crown of science, of art, and of poetry. She has taken under her patronage these three, the proudest and the freest in the world, and accompanied by them, she marches on through history in dazzling glory and magnificence. In accordance with the wish of the dying Nicholas V, expressed in a discourse which seems to express the mind of this great Pope and his like better than any other document, she subjugates the human imagination and compels admiration by the incomparable prestige of her aesthetic greatness.

One feels this deeply when at Rome, under the lofty cupola which shelters the tomb of the Fisherman of men and from which shines forth in gigantic letters this divine sentence: "Thou art Peter, and upon this rock I will build my Church." No one, I think, can wholly escape the spell of these surroundings: neither the Christian who feels his heart expand, nor the indifferent one who finds again a remnant of Catholic joy and pride, nor the dissenter who must feel in his inmost heart a melancholy regret for the broken unity of the ancient Christian faith. As to the enemies of the Church, however intense their hatred, however vicious the blows they deal her, they feel here more than elsewhere the presence of Him Who has said: "The wicked shall see, and shall be angry, he shall gnash with his teeth and pine away: the desire of the wicked shall perish."

*Importance of stand taken by Church at this turning point of history.*

This is, I think, the aspect under which we must consider the role of the Church and of the papacy at this turning point of history, known as the Renaissance. I am aware that this is not the opinion of everyone. There are today many people, especially among the best Christians and among those who aim to restore Catholic inspiration to art and poetry, who regret the great part taken by the Church in the work of the Renaissance. They think that she protected the humanists and the artists more than she should have done, that she did not safeguard the tradition of Catholic art and Catholic thought against the new ideas, and that she needlessly sacrificed to the taste of the time the elements of Christian vitality. They would almost picture paganism invading the sanctuaries and making the Church of Christ the prisoner of the age.

And certainly, as I have hinted above, there is no lack of circumstances to give to this judgment an appearance of truth. By bringing together all the data furnished by the shocking chronicles of the sixteenth century, in Rome as elsewhere, by gathering such sayings and such actions of princes of the Church as were manifestly opposed to the law of God, it would be easy to paint a picture which would call forth strong condemnation. But likewise, one might take the opposite elements and picture a society worthy of the first centuries of Christianity. But history need not resort to special pleading.

The truth is that if the Church, in face of the widespread intellectual movement whose origin and character we have considered, had confined herself to protest and reaction and had wrapped herself in tradition as does the vanquished soldier in the folds of his flag, she would have permitted civilization to leave her behind; she would have lost all contact with the future and would have had no influence upon the elite of mankind; she would have become a closed chapel where the faithful – dwindling in numbers day by day – would meet only to weep over ruins and to anathematize the age. We should be thankful that she resisted the temptation and that, thanks to the wisdom of the Popes, she rose to the height of the movement of the sixteenth century, that she has remained abreast of the times down to the twentieth century, and that she will not fail to keep pace with all the movements of future ages. The essential point is that, in throwing open her sanctuaries to the new intellectual life of mankind, she did not sacrifice a particle of the higher truth, a single commandment of the moral law, a single article of her creed. No doubt, it was difficult at times to reconcile the severe requirements of the eternal laws with the bold movements of the modern spirit, and often the moralist and the lover of the beautiful must have been shocked at the poorly veiled contradictions which resulted from the union of the Church and the Renaissance. But it is nonetheless true that the Church of the sixteenth century has handed down intact the patrimony of primitive Christianity.

An anecdote which I read for the first time in the beautiful *History of the Popes* by Pastor presents this thought in so expressive a manner that I cannot resist the pleasure of repeating it as the crowning point of this lecture.

Julius II, as you all know, had asked Bramante, the greatest and boldest genius of the Renaissance, to re-build the Basilica of St. Peter on the Vatican Hill. Bramante combined boundless faith in the principles of his art with contempt of the past – a failing common to nearly all the artists of that epoch. He began by demolishing the ancient Vatican Basilica which, it is true, threatened to collapse, but he acted with a haste and lack of respect that were inexcusable. In the boldness of his genius, he went even further. In order to make the new church more imposing, he wished to change its orientation and, for his purpose, he thought of moving the tomb which, for fifteen centuries, has been the inviolate asylum of the sacred remains of the Prince of the Apostles. But on this point Pope Julius II, who so far had granted every request of his artist, gave a categorical refusal. Bramante would not be silenced; he brought forward a number of reasons, some from considerations of art, others from the viewpoint of religion. He contended that if the tomb were moved as he desired it would be in better harmony with the enlarged edifice and would add to the piety of the faithful; in a word, he used every argument and pleaded with a vehemence and an obstinacy which seemed likely to triumph in the end. But the Pope was inexorable; he declared that under no consideration would he allow anyone to touch the tomb of him upon whom Jesus Christ had built the universal Church. Art had to give way to religion. The remains of St. Peter were not taken from their crypt and the orientation of the church was not changed.

This story is significant. It tells friends and enemies alike that the Catholic Church accommodates herself to all progress of thought and to all forms of art, but that built upon the rock of the eternal truths – she permits no one to change the axis of the world which she has set towards Heaven.

Chapter VII

# THE CHURCH AND THE REVOLUTION

On May 5, 1789, there convened at Versailles the States-General of France.[77] Surely no one could have then foretold that within less than five years royalty would be suppressed, that the king and queen would be put to death, that the dauphin would die a slow death in a cobbler's shop, that the nobility would have to choose between the guillotine and exile, that the Catholic religion would be proscribed, that a girl of the demi-monde would ascend the altar of Notre Dame of Paris under the name of Goddess of Reason and that, among the deputies who took part in the procession, there would be one, the most ridiculous, the most awkward, and perhaps the most shallow of them all, who would cut the throats of most of his colleagues. Had such a prediction been made, it would have met with derision and indignation. This series of unlikely suppositions, dramatized after their occurrence by La Harpe, in his famous *Prédication de Cazotte*, falls far short of the frightful realities which sank the ancient regime into an abyss of blood.

*Revolution unforeseen.*

There had been nothing to foretell the awful catastrophe to the generation which witnessed those scenes unprecedented in the annals of history. Apart from certain black specks which could forebode no evil except to the most trained eye, the sky was serene and the morrow seemed favorable. The dynasty was popular; this had been very evident at the birth of the dauphin. The election records of 1789 attest that the immense majority of voters were sincerely devoted to religion and to royalty alike. It is true that various reforms were demanded; but all these, or almost all, had to do with undeniable abuses, which were no longer defended by any one, not even by those who profited by them. And then the gentleness of manners was such that there was nothing to fear even from the most energetic reformers. Every one boasted of being a sensible man, just as in other times, one would have been ashamed of it. Literature, that supreme authority of the epoch, took more and more the character of the idyll. An atmosphere of benevolence seemed about to envelop and permeate all society. People had acquired such reliance in the native goodness of humanity and in the excellence of the principles of philosophy that they loved to think of the future under the aspect of a golden age, which they believed they were about to attain. The first measures of the Constituent Assembly,[78] voted by acclamation and often on the motion of the privileged classes themselves, were not such as to open the eyes of men. The Feast of the Federation (July 14, 1790) was, in this respect, a real illusion. Every one believed that the pact of human fraternity had been sealed on the basis of liberty. The error was of long duration. They were still exchanging love kisses long after claps of thunder had been heard in the peaceful sky. Even the imagination of the sinister cut-throats held fast to the vision of the great human pastoral. It was in an azure-colored garment, with a sheaf of ears of grain and flowers in hand, that the sensible Robespierre,[79] the eloquent opponent of capital punishment, was to celebrate the feast of the Supreme Being on an altar in mid-air. He dreamed, no doubt, of the welfare of the human race, of the sweetness of country life, of the charms of virtue and innocence – and this but a few days before the frightful awakening of the ninth of Thermidor!

*Purpose of Revolution destruction of ancient regime.*

If conditions were such, how explain this atrocious Revolution, this hideous debauch, whither sacrilegious folly and sanguinary impiety led dismayed humanity for years? How understand this vertigo which, at a given moment, took hold of the first nation of the world, and made it turn round and round and stagger like a drunken man, and so affected it that up to the present it has not recovered its former stability? Are these the necessary crises which accompany the bringing forth of a new world? Are they the agonizing convulsions of an ancient civilization? Are they the tragic phases of that gigantic struggle between two powers which is going on forever for the possession of society – the struggle between good and evil, between truth and error, between God and Satan?

Certainly it would be idle to attribute the Revolution to the abuses of the ancient regime. It would be assigning a most insignificant cause to an effect whose proportions are almost beyond calculation. There have been abuses at all times, and when the French Revolution burst forth there were abuses elsewhere as well as in France. But there was not everywhere else, as in France, a most sincere goodwill, on the part of the ruling classes, to extirpate abuses. Louis XVI, who was called *the best of kings*, set the example in this respect. He restored to the Protestants their civil rights, he suppressed the rack, he convened the Assembly of the Notables,[80] and when, finally, he took the initiative in calling together the States-General (which had not been in session since 1614) it was to bring about the collaboration of the king and his people in working out the necessary reforms. There was the same goodwill, the same sincerity among the two privileged classes, namely the clergy and the nobility. They both generously sacrificed their most precious prerogatives for the sake of public peace and the general welfare, the clergy with spontaneous resignation, the nobility with rather thoughtless enthusiasm. Never before had privileged classes renounced their privileges for reasons of patriotism and philosophy. It may be said that if the Revolution had risen to do away with abuses, it would have come to a close after the night of the Fourth of August, 1789, that is, when it had hardly begun.

It is therefore false to pretend that the Revolution was caused by the abuses of the ancient regime. The Revolution was more than a mere effort to resist abuses which had ceased to exist before it triumphed. Its purpose – if it had a purpose at all – was not the reform of the regime, but its destruction. A blind irresistible force, it acted with all the power of a furious element let loose and it overthrew society from top to bottom, uprooting everything after the manner of a cyclone, leaving the ground strewn with ruins wherever it had passed. But, as in meteorology one may give reasons for the appearance of cyclones, so also, in history, the outburst of similar catastrophes may be traced to its causes.

## THE CHURCH AT THE TURNING POINTS OF HISTORY

*Free thought one of the causes of Revolution.*
The revolutionary spirit is far anterior to the Revolution. In France, as elsewhere, one may trace it back to the Renaissance from which it proceeds as the river flows from the glacier. The Renaissance, as we have seen, had developed two parallel currents whose junction, at a given moment, had become the great destructive force. The first current, that of free thought, held course among the cultured classes; the other, that of free enjoyment, had its source in high society. For a long time, the freethinkers held aloof, with disdainful indifference for the great religious struggles. They saw in these nothing but the quarrels of bigots, and when they became involved in them, it was to strike with the weapon of irony the one of the two combatants who at the time appeared the more formidable. Christianity under all its forms inspired them with equal aversion. Their admiration went out only to pagan antiquity, which had neither dogmas to bridle the mind nor priesthood to interpret its dogmas. Encamped on the field of pure naturalism, they waited the moment when Protestantism, which unconsciously had prepared the way for them, would have finished beating down the buttresses of the temple, that they might then hurl themselves against the noble edifice with sap and hammer.

Being revolutionaries of a special kind, they did not oppose the civil power to any great extent, first because they saw in royal absolutism a fair realization of their ideal of pagan politics, also because they were not eager for martyrdom. The spirit of free thought did not yield to the movement of the Catholic Restoration which marked so brilliantly the opening annals of the seventeenth century; but flowed beneath as an undercurrent and finally reappeared to be denounced by the thundering voice of Bossuet,[81] at the threshold of the eighteenth century. Then it emptied its filthy waters upon a world prepared to receive it. It then made up for its long enforced silence. From Fontenelle, who said that he would not open his hand even were it full of truth, to Bayle who opened wide a hand filled with sophisms and lies, the distance is not perceptible from the viewpoint of chronology but, for him who looks beneath the surface, what a road was travelled between *L'Histoire des Oracles*, published by Fontenelle in 1687, and the *Dictionnaire Philosophique* by Bayle, which appeared in 1697! In the former we have still the elegant skepticism of the man of the world, who slips a discreet doubt in a happy phrase, in a good word, in a smile; in the latter we have open and cynical unbelief in all its brutality. As has been aptly remarked, all Voltaire is found in the *Dictionnaire Philosophique*. The role of the patriot of Ferney consisted in popularizing the philosophy of Bayle and in giving it a militant and aggressive character.

*Licentiousness another cause of Revolution.*

Along with unbelief there grew up licentiousness of morals. Bred in high society, where man no longer saw anything in life but a round of pleasure, it had contaminated the entire court of the Valois, and we find shameful traces of it in the well-known physiognomy of the Béarnais. Think of the morals of that society of which Brantome in the sixteenth century and Hamilton in the seventeenth century were the complaisant chroniclers! One is shocked at the cynicism and the frivolity with which men and women rushed headlong in the pursuit of the most unavowable pleasures. So long as Louis XIV lived, the prestige he gave to his reign concealed all these turpitudes under the broad folds of the royal purple, and men showed some decency, some respect of self and of others, even amid the most revolting excesses; but his death gave the signal for an unprecedented loosening of all moral restraint. I should offend my hearers, were I to indicate, even in the most discreet manner, the example set by the Regent and by Louis XV; but it must be said that it was followed very generally and that, with a few honorable exceptions, high society seemed anxious to make all France the home of wickedness. Never had Christian civilization witnessed so shameful a spectacle.

*Unbelief and licentiousness fostered by Voltaire.*

The two currents above mentioned had more than once mixed their muddy waters during the long years which preceded the advent of Voltaire; with him they became finally but the one current which was about to flood France. It was at the hotel of the Temple, among the leaders of vice and impiety who then held their headquarters there, that the sinister pontiff of modern irreligion grew up. This friend of the *libertines* of high society was also on good terms with the notorious Ninon de Lenclos, who bequeathed to him two thousand francs for the purchase of books. It affords some satisfaction to know that the greatest enemy of the Christian faith should have been the protégé of a courtesan. For my part, when I consider that the "philosophy" comes to us from the boudoir of Ninon, I feel as did Tertullian who congratulated himself on the fact that the first persecutor of Christianity was Nero.

Voltaire was the most complete incarnation of the irreligious spirit of the eighteenth century. To the French corruption and frivolity he added the hateful fanaticism which he imbibed, while in England, from the deists of that country. After his return he was perhaps the most marvellous workman of destruction who has ever appeared. He was endowed with a mind unequalled in suppleness and vivacity, universally gifted as a writer, skilled in the infernal art of handling the poisonous weapon of sarcasm and irony; and, in the war to death which he had declared against Christianity, he employed all the resources of a mind exceptionally constituted for intellectual struggles and all the indefatigable activities of a satanic hatred against the Church. For almost a century, he led the irreligious campaign with astounding obstinacy and – to use the expression of a great modern poet – he was the missionary of the devil among the men of his time. He is little read nowadays, because, notwithstanding his prodigious talent, his works were of his day; nevertheless his mind remains the evil genius of the modern world, and, to the present day, the Christian cannot look upon his hideous likeness without feelings of fright and horror.

Gathered about Voltaire were all the defenders of impiety, or "philosophy," as they were pleased then to designate it. From this crowd came forth the *Encyclopédie*, a formidable engine of war which, under the pretext of presenting to the public a summary of modern knowledge, carried to all classes hatred and contempt of Christianity. *Ecrasez l'infâme!* (Crush the infamous thing!) was the watchword of the master; the disciples often outstripped their master. They found him bigoted, for they were atheists, while Voltaire honored God by believing in Him. Banded together as organized leaders of public opinion, surrounded by the prestige of science, and winning fresh popularity from the mild opposition of the civil power, the Encyclopedists were able to undermine with impunity all religious belief, all the foundations of moral and social life. They succeeded, moreover, in enlisting the co-operation of the civil power in their work. Revolutionaries in religious matters, they were, at least apparently, conservatives in politics. *Bold against God alone*, they knew how to spare the despots, how to glorify them when necessary. Were not the kings who hated religion the best of kings? This is why Voltaire cringed before Frederick II,[82] before Catherine II,[83] even before Madame de Pompadour, the notorious mistress of King Louis XV, indifferent as he was to everything save his combat against the faith of Jesus Christ. Provided he were given control of religion, nothing else concerned him, as he realized, no doubt, that this was all he needed. It would appear that at times, in the midst of his work of death, he caught a glimpse of what was to happen: "After me, they will see a fine racket," he wrote. This, however, was but a flash, and he went back at once to his accursed work.

*Seductive theories of Rousseau impelling factor.*

But if Voltaire did not draw political conclusions because he was too much in love with his own ease, and because, in the main, he was still imbued with the ancient regime, there was one who was willing to draw these conclusions for him. This one, unlike the great lord who wished to die quietly in his beautiful solitude at Ferney, was a soured plebeian, ill-bred, suspicious, a misanthrope to a degree. Possessing the soul of a poet and the heart of a footman, Jean Jacques Rousseau hated and despised the society in which he lived, the civilization which surrounded him, all society and all civilization. He had all that was needed to make his revolutionary passions penetrate into the hearts of others: captivating warmth of expression, genuine sensibility, sincere emotion, enthusiasm for the good and the beautiful, or for what he believed to be such. He introduced a new strain into French literature. To the artificial society of the salons, he, the savage who had slept under the open sky, revealed the charms of nature; he gave a taste for the beauties of the landscape to the great lords who had never seen one except through the windows of their castles; at his voice, the entire court rose to go with Queen Marie Antoinette to contemplate the early dawn. Even Voltaire had his hour of infatuation!

Nevertheless, these are not the real triumphs of Jean Jacques. He had made far different discoveries in his musings as a lone walker. He had discovered that man is good when he comes from the hand of nature but becomes corrupted when he lives in the state of society. This is a heresy with an added sophism, because it denies original sin, and what is society but man? He had discovered that all the arts of civilization, and particularly science and literature, serve but to increase corruption. He had discovered that society is the result of a contract between its members and that the source of law is their will, which may express itself whenever it pleases. Away with religion, with morality, with tradition! The people are the only sovereign, and any institution, any law, any will opposed to the people is tyranny, usurpation, and high treason.

These were the political theories of Rousseau[84] which his eloquence and enthusiasm succeeded in fastening upon the minds of his contemporaries. A society which had been taught to scoff at the religious law and to believe in nothing was to accept with enthusiasm such seductive theories: accordingly the doctrine of the *Contrat Social* became in a short time the doctrine of the cultured public. The disciples of Rousseau were legion, chiefly among the classes whom the sarcasms of Voltaire had turned away from religion and who, having ceased to believe in the Christian ideal, could not do without some kind of ideal and thought they had found it in the dreamings of the sophist of Geneva.

But is it really true that the alliance between free thought and voluptuousness is sufficient to bring forth the revolutionary spirit? Is it not true that elsewhere – as in England – the ruling classes had displayed, with no less cynicism than in France, their contempt for the Christian faith and the moral law? Still England did not cease to be the most conservative nation in the world. This is true, and it would be interesting to follow closely the energetic reaction whereby the English people rid themselves of their own philosophers in order to come back to Christian tradition. But, without taking into account the fact that the evil was more deeply rooted in France, one must not forget that France is the land where all ideas tend to be at once translated into facts: in France less than elsewhere do people tolerate the contradiction between the ideal and the reality. And the French cultured classes had their ideal of political society, which had been elaborated by the

Renaissance and perfected by the philosophy of the eighteenth century. This ideal, borrowed from ancient literature and adapted to modern society, was a dream of the imagination, an abstract conception evolved from pure reason; nothing seemed more urgent or more easy than the realization of this ideal. All that seemed necessary was to put it into effect by law and thus bring down to earth liberty, civic virtue, reason, philosophy and universal felicity.

Thus they thought. They were far removed from that faith in religion and in country which had caused Jean Racine[85] to write that truly Gallican sentence: "God has given me the grace never to be ashamed either of my king or of the Gospel." On the contrary, they were convinced that religion and monarchy or, as they expressed it, fanaticism and despotism caused all the evils of humanity. They thought that humanity – duped by priests and crushed by tyrants – would rise to the height of its glorious mission only when it would rid itself of priest and tyrant and give ear only to the teachings of philosophy. We have already spoken of the enthusiastic hope with which the sensible heart of the philosophers and their disciples looked forward to the glad day. We must add that all obstacles to the realization of their golden dream, all reaction against the generous efforts they made for the public welfare enraged these gentle and humane mortals. They considered every opposition a monstrous attempt against human liberty; and there was no punishment which, in their anger, they did not dream of inflicting on the criminal author. For their "philosophy" was a religion; and if it did not send its heretics to the funeral pyre, because of their horror of the Inquisition, it found other means of chastisement for contemnors of its orthodoxy. By way of anticipation, we may say that this is all that the Revolution really discovered.

*Philosophers put theories into practice – Revolution accomplished.*

It is true that the philosophers and their pupils were not the nation. But they were its moving and active spirit, and, as is always the case, it was easy to have others mistake them for the nation. They were loud of speech; though without authority, they spoke in the name of the people and made themselves heard more and more every day; they kept telling the people, as Sieyès expressed it, that they had been nothing and that they were to be everything. And scarcely had the States-General reassembled when the philosophers took possession of the assembly in the name of the nation, and pretended that the other orders had no right and that the king was merely their mandatory. Louis XVI had imprudently taken the stand that the States-General should vote by Orders, whilst the Third Estate wished that they should cast individual votes. At once it was evident that the will of the Third Estate placed itself above the will of the king. When the master of ceremonies enjoined the Third Estate to go to their own assembly hall and leave that of the general meeting, President Bailly replied: "I hold that the assembled nation cannot be commanded." This saying, more authentic than the one attributed to Mirabeau, is also much more expressive: the one, on the lips of the tribune, was the unauthorized whim of a factionist; the other, in the mouth of the President of the Third Estate, modest in its form but haughty in meaning, expressed the usurpation of all power by the people.

The Revolution was accomplished. The events which followed were but the logical development of this opening. And, if thirst for blood and love of noise were not an integral part of the revolutionary spirit, then it would be on June 23, 1789, and not on July 14, that the leaders of the France of today should celebrate the anniversary of their emancipation.

Thus was the ancient regime delivered entirely into the hands of the States-General. They did with it as they pleased and left to the king only the doubtful privilege of endorsing their work, under the penalty of new riots. The "philosophers" were the masters of France. At last reason was to reign.

*Poor showing of lawmakers.*

But reason was to make a poor showing and the lawmakers were destined to fall far short of their task. As a whole, they formed a body singularly inexperienced and awkward, and at the same time presumptuous, in face of the gigantic task undertaken. Away from politics for centuries, the States-General did not know how to conduct associations of men. They were reformers in theory; they believed that the welfare of humanity could be enacted by laws, and they naïvely legislated patriotism and national happiness. As already stated, most of them were filled with classical recollections and impressed with the idea of the republican virtues which, in their student days, they had admired in the heroes of antiquity. They recalled these memories and enacted laws like college boys. Is there anything in the whole history of civilization more grotesque and at the same time more pitiable than the action of Hérault de Séchelles, President of the Convention, who, when they were about to draw up one of the many constitutions which the Revolutionaries gave to France, sent to the National Library for the laws of Minos,[86] in order to transcribe from them the laws he intended to give his country?

No wonder that the force of events, the laws of history, the laws of common sense should work havoc with the theses of Rousseau. Scarcely had the States-General informed the king that the people were the only sovereign, when there arose from the crowd a thousand threatening voices repeating to them what they had said to the king: "We are the sovereign people and you are but our mandatories!"

*Revolutionary leaders overthrown.*

And who spoke thus? Was it really the people of France? Not at all! The people were at their firesides, in the shops, behind the plough, engaged in fruitful and civilizing work; they had recorded their wishes in the election of 1789 and, whenever they were given an opportunity to express their will, they disavowed the intriguers and the malefactors who presumed to speak in their name. But what did these care? There being no longer any master in France – since on the fourteenth of July and the fifth of October, 1789, they had put aside the royal authority – they felt that they were the true masters of their country. They were organized, they knew what they wanted, they had under their thumb the king and the States-General against whom they could at pleasure incite well-planned riots; at one stroke they made June 20, August 10, May 31, the great revolutionary dates. It was in the clubs that they worked out the popular movements. In these clubs the most fanatical and the most unscrupulous were in control, and, in the last analysis, two or three men – and these the worst of their kind – were the real sovereign people.

Taine, the well-known French critic and historian, in characterizing the triumvirate which controlled the destinies of France, has said that it was composed of a madman – Marat,[87] of a savage – Danton,[88] and of a pedant – Robespierre. These are the true sons of Voltaire and of Rousseau. Robespierre took the *Contrat Social* as his gospel; he had no other political education. With a handful of accomplices, these wretches went to work with no other aim, with no other ideal than to beat down all that stood in their way; everything fell before them: first, the kings, nobles and priests, then all others who did not share their revolutionary ideal, all who were *moderantist,* as they put it in their jargon, the Feuillants,[89] the Girondists,[90] until having levelled all else – they set out to destroy one another. The Jacobins[91] cut the throats of the Cordeliers,[92] the Thermidorians[93] cut the throats of the Jacobins, the Directory[94] deported the rest. Finally there came a dictator who, amid the plaudits of France, drove out the whole menagerie at the crack of the whip, and re-established for his own benefit the much despised despotism. The last revolutionaries became his footmen and his courtiers; he gave them golden liveries with which they were well pleased and one of them, having become a prince of the Empire, said to his old comrades of the Montagne[95]: "In public, be sure to call me Your Excellency, but among ourselves call me simply Monseigneur."[96]

This is amusing, no doubt, and the enemies of the Revolution may find amusement at seeing the tragedy end in a farce. But what is more serious is the fact that, before making honorable amends in the ante-chambers of the new Caesar, the revolutionary spirit had time to invade all Europe and to spread everywhere the evil germ from which we suffer to the present day. The evil of the Revolution is the pretension to treat political society as if it were the creation of pure reason, independent of the action of the divine laws which rule the life of the world and of humanity!

This, in a few words, is the origin of the French Revolution. Long before its realization it was in the minds and the hearts of men; its success was brought about by the abdication, or complicity, of all the forces which should have opposed it. It was the breaking out of the malady at once intellectual and moral which for a long time had been working on the nation, coming down from the ruling classes to the rank and file of the citizens where it was transformed into a political catastrophe.

*Revolution could have been avoided.*

Could this catastrophe have been avoided?

Unhesitatingly I answer yes, and I add that it would have been avoided if the Catholic Church had been there. But the Church was not there to help France. The Church, from the time of the fourteenth century, had been excluded from the political councils; it had been looked upon by the kings as a stranger – even as a rival; it had been enslaved to the point of having to sacrifice the Society of Jesus to the importunities of Freemasonry[97]; it had been deprived of its rights so that it was no longer allowed to teach the doctrine of the infallibility of the Sovereign Pontiff; it had been watched and tracked even in its liturgy; so that the Church in France was nothing more than one of the wheels put in motion by the despotism of the State. The Gallican Church had permitted the lay power to impose upon it the doctrine of the four articles, which was a bold encroachment of the State upon an exclusively doctrinal domain. She received at the hands of the king dogmas which she rejected from the hand of the Pope. It was of no benefit to her that she formed a privileged Order; this condition, favorable on the surface, was an incessant source of loss and unpopularity. Associated, as she was, with the destinies of the civil power, she became conjointly liable and public opinion held her responsible for all the mistakes of the regime of which she was a part. She was out of contact with the public spirit, had at her disposal no lever to move the minds of men, and was without influence in the world of ideas.

It was unfortunate that all dignitaries of the Church were chosen exclusively from the nobility, at a time when the nobility had fallen into general disfavor. At one time – the time of Louis XIV – there had been in the ranks of the higher clergy some children of the bourgeoisie who did not cut so bad a figure on episcopal thrones – one of these was Bossuet. But when the revolution burst forth, among the hundred and thirty bishops of the kingdom of Franks, there was not one plebeian! Taken as a whole, the episcopate was commendable in private life and was not wanting in good qualities; but what a gulf between it and the nation, what a source of misunderstanding! The higher clergy – noble, attached to the court, absentees, worldly, almost laicized – did not rise to the occasion: they had neither the prestige of learning, nor the éclat of great virtue, nor the advantage of real popularity: they were not the kind to guide the Church through the tempests.

Nor were the inferior clergy more abreast of the times. True, they gave the example of Christian virtue, and stood intact in a gangrened society. Tocqueville gives this magnificent testimonial: "I began the study of the ancient society filled with prejudices against it, I finished it filled with respect." Other witnesses speak in the same manner and everyone knows the heroism of the French clergy in weathering the stormy days of the Revolution. But, if they were well preserved from a moral point of view, they no longer had the true notion of the full part they were to play in society. They languished in a general state of dejection, they were resigned to be nothing, they did not protest when they saw the Church humiliated. As a keen observer[98] has remarked, they lacked *intellectual courage* and were, in a word, more ready for martyrdom than for the apostolate. And what is still worse, a great many of them, ignorant of the beauty of the social doctrine of Catholicism, allowed themselves to be won over by the doctrine of Rousseau; and they applauded, as if these were discoveries made by the philosophers, the few particles of truth which were really Catholic doctrine. To such an extent had the social and political traditions been obliterated even among the clergy! I know of nothing so painful as the illusion of those pastors who – the guardians of a treasure – allow counterfeit money to be substituted for the genuine coin!

Thus, the most heartrending spectacle of that whole century was not the deafening cries of error and crime but the silence of the Catholic Church concerning social truth. All lying doctrines were heard – but the Church of God was dumb. Her voice was the only one which did not rise in the din of discordant voices which characterizes the eighteenth century as noisy and strange. The century listened in vain for a teacher endowed with authority and eloquence to propound the luminous and sound teachings of the Catholic Faith on the nature of society, on the mission of the State and of the civic powers. These lofty ideas were the only ones without defenders, but there was no sophism which did not find as advocate some man of talent or of genius.

Do we appreciate what would have happened if, during the ages which saw the apogee of the monarchy, there had arisen bishops, priests and laymen to proclaim the eternal social principles of Christianity – who, going beyond the Renaissance to the great doctors of the Middle Ages, would have taught an astonished world that there is such a thing as Christian politics not to be confounded with the politics of royal absolutism, but which contains at once the eternal truths and their applications, *nova et vetera*? Do we realize what would have happened if, like Fénelon in his *Plan de Gouvernement* written for the Duke of Burgundy, they had protested against the enslavement of the Church, demanded for her *freedom as in Turkey*,[99] preached the suppression of the unbridled luxury of the court, branded all abuses and sought means to remedy the evils of society? May we not believe that they would have been heeded? Would not the destinies of the world have been changed if, when the problem of social re-organization arose, there had been found an episcopate to recall to the world that the solution of the problem should be sought in the Gospel and in Catholic doctrine, instead of seeking it in *L'Esprit des Lois*[100] and in the *Contrat Social*? If the Church had spoken with her authority in all questions where the welfare of humanity was at stake, what light would she not have shed on the darkness of the controversies touching the mission of the State and of society? Think of the resources the Church would have brought to all the generous and sincere leaders who, at the beginning of the Revolution, dreamed of a free and rejuvenated France under the aegis of religion and under the authority of the king! The nation would have had its political creed to oppose to the innovators, and the divorce which the sophists succeeded in bringing about between religion and the friends of liberty would have had no reason to exist. The espousal by the men of those days of the false maxims of the Revolution was possible only because of the silence of the gagged and powerless Church; it would have been prevented by churchmen conscious of their mission and enjoying the fullness of freedom.

Since then, if I may use the expression, the Catholic Church has once more become herself. One might have thought that she slept at the time of the Revolution; but it was the sleep of Jesus in the bark shaken by the tempest. Her awakening, tardy though it may seem, has been all the more fruitful. A great intellectual and social movement is already under way in the ranks of the Church:- it is the beginning of the great struggle – the greatest of all her struggles against the powers of darkness.

Let us not make the same mistake and be deceived by appearances. Our own atmosphere is not less charged than was that of the Revolution. I dare say that even the Revolution was not preceded by symptoms as formidable as those which now, under our eyes, seem to foreshadow a new catastrophe. In our day, we would not smile at the prediction of another Cazotte tracing, as he did at the end of the eighteenth century, a dark and hopeless picture of the future.

*New awakening of Christian society.*

But, let us not forget that the condition of the Christian world has been greatly changed in the course of a century. Then the revolutionary spirit was young, bubbling with life; its hands were filled with promises of endless happiness; it was master of the earth; all humanity welcomed it; the forces of social conservation surrendered to it. But today it is old and decrepit; its prevarication is as clear as the light of day; condemned by all thinking men, it is no longer anything but a superstition believed in only by mediocre minds. At that time the Catholic Church, mutilated and enslaved, was a captive whom the catastrophe found prostrate at the foot of the throne, awaiting her turn to mount the scaffold. Today, freed and herself again, she rises a giant and faces Revolution, not only to defend the domains which still are hers but also to recover those of which she has been despoiled. She has shattered all the maxims of philosophism. She has recalled to life the Society of Jesus whose suppression had been forced on her.[101] She has proclaimed the infallibility of her head. In 1832 and in 1864 she condemned the false doctrine of 1789. Finally, building again on the ruins of the city of lies, she has proclaimed in immortal encyclicals the Christian Constitution of States and the Magna Carta of the emancipation of labor.

Who will deny that today, as in the Middle Ages, the Catholic Church is the highest authority? She speaks to all humanity in an accent sweet and strong and all her own. And she alone can talk to mankind. Amid the universal crash of thrones and schools and doctrines, she is the one moral force which remains standing and her astonishing superiority is enhanced by the very depth of their fall. She has but to raise her voice and from all parts of the universe she is answered. Today there is such a thing as Catholic thought, which measures all things by the rule of Christian truth, condemning what is opposed to it, accepting what is not hostile. Strong and respected, conscious of its power, it circulates from one end of the world to the other; no longer can any sophism withstand it. In sociology, in science, in art, in all manifestations of the intellectual and moral life of the people, Catholic thought asserts itself with increasing force and energy. It is not refuted because it is irrefutable; it is opposed only by the conspiracy of silence.

Nor is this all. Descending from the field of doctrine to that of action, the Catholic spirit has taken possession of public life. The Catholic battalions are re-organized; on every side, an army of laymen is rising. The people come to uphold their clergy; the rank and file of the faithful insist on sharing the struggle. How cheering it is, in time of trouble, to see the recruits rally about their banner! The work is indeed long and tedious, but nothing can prevent its accomplishment! It is going on in different countries – in Belgium, in Holland, in Catholic Germany, in Northern Italy; in other countries persecution must act as a spur to the tardy ones. And he would be blind indeed who would fail to see in the fury and stubbornness of persecutors the expiring effort of iniquity!

The triumph of the Catholic cause is secure, even from a human point of view. Today, as at all critical stages of her growth, she has displayed the same marvellous adaptability. Detaching her cause from that of any class that might seek to identify itself with her, she has answered them as she answered the Jews, as she answered Feudalism, as she answered all the ghosts of the past. She lets the dead bury their dead and enters into compact with the twentieth century. She lays out a course for the rising masses. It is not the course of the Revolution – as her slanderers say – it is the program of the Gospel, the program of St. Thomas of Aquin.[102] It is the welcoming of all by the Kingdom of God, disregarding birth and wealth, considering only merit and virtue; it is the democracy of the Gospel built upon the poor and where we see realized the law of justice and fraternity in an ever widening application of the great *New Commandment.*

She opposes to the bloody and sinister ideals of the red flag and the cap of the convict her incomparable ideal of the love of God and the love of man, with its symbol of the Cross. Despite all contrary appearances we need not doubt of her final triumph. The human soul is naturally Christian; everything great and good gravitates towards the Gospel. Human society is drawn instinctively in the direction of Jesus Christ whenever it obeys the laws of self-preservation. The spirit of evil may do its worst, it will but precipitate events and hasten the day when humanity will have choice only between Catholic civilization and revolutionary anarchy. And then the choice will soon be made.

Let us then greet with hope and respect the progress that is going on at this moment in Christian society. It is a new Catholic spring-time. We have seen other spectacles of the kind in our study of the Church in the past. They must help us to appreciate what is now going on under our eyes, affording, as they do, a new proof of the indefectible vitality of the Church. We would indeed be blind to the teachings of history were we, at this stage of her life, to forget that now, as in the past, she is upholding not the interests of a class but the cause of humanity.

# NOTES

1. Stilicho, a brave Vandal, shared in the military exploits of Emperor Theodosius (379 – 395), twice defeated Alaric, king of the Visigoths, and compelled him to abandon Italy. In 405 he conquered the German tribes which had invaded Italy under the leadership of the Ostrogoth, Radahais.

2. Aetius was the son of an Italian mother and Gaudentius, a Scythian soldier of the Empire. In the summer of 450 Aetius, in concert with the brave and loyal Theodoric, king of the Ostrogoths, relieved Orléans besieged by Atilla, and arrested the progress of the great Hun on the Catalaunian Fields, near Troyes, where he won one of the decisive victories of history and saved Europe for Latins, Teutons, Celts and Slavs, against the degraded and odious Huns.

3. Ataulph, brother and successor to Alaric, chieftain of the Visigoths, pillaged Rome, but later became reconciled with the Emperor and was commissioned to drive the Barbarians from Spain. He was assassinated at Barcelona before he had completed his task.

4. Theodoric the Great, descendant of the royal Ostrogoth family of the Amali. At eighteen, in 489, he led a great horde of his countrymen into Italy, where he destroyed the kingdom of Odoacer in 495 and became the sole ruler of Italy.

5. Since this was written, the events which have taken place or which are in preparation in the extreme Orient may have modified the ideas of some. If I mistake not, everyone is not absolutely convinced of the impossibility of a new Atilla or a new Genghis Khan, who, equipped with the perfected tools of modern warfare, might throw upon the Western World five hundred million men of the yellow races.

6. See Author's *Introduction to Clovis,* 2 edit, vol. I, p. XXV.

7. The Arians were followers of Arius, a priest of Alexandria in Egypt, who denied the divinity of Christ. Arianism spread far and wide. Arian kingdoms arose in Spain, Africa, Italy. Arianism was condemned at the Council of Nicaea, near Constantinople, in 325 and became extinguished before the eighth century.

8. Clovis, (466 – 511), the founder of the Merovingian line of Frankish kings, married the Christian princess Clotilda in 493, defeated the Alemanni in 496. He was baptised by Saint Remigius the same year in fulfilment of a vow made in battle to the God of Clotilda. As in the case of Constantine the Great the baptism of Clovis led to a rapid diffusion of the Christian religion among his subjects.

9. Constantine the Great, son of Constantine Chlorus joint-emperor with Galerius,

# THE CHURCH AT THE TURNING POINTS OF HISTORY

in 312 marched upon Maxentius, the worthless ruler of Rome, and defeated him in the battle of the Milvian Bridge. Before this battle, according to the testimony of Constantine, as recorded by Eusebius a contemporaneous historian, a fiery cross appeared in the sky with this inscription: *In touto nika*. ("In this sign conquer.") Constantine publicly ascribed the victory to the God of the Christians and was the first Roman Emperor to receive Christian baptism.

10. St. Boniface, Apostle of Germany, Benedictine monk, was born in England, May 15, 719. Pope Gregory II gave him full authority to preach the Gospel to the heathens in Germany to the right of the Rhine. When he saw the great results of his labours, he returned to Rome in 722, and was consecrated bishop. Ten years later he was appointed Archbishop with authority to set up bishoprics among the peoples he converted. He drew upon a code of laws for the government of the Church in the country. When he had finished his work in Germany he undertook to evangelize the Frisians by whom he was martyred.

11. Charlemagne (742 – 814), Emperor of the West and King of France, was a great patron of letters. Under his reign, notwithstanding continual wars, he established schools throughout his empire. He invited from England Alcuin (A.D. 804), a distinguished scholar and pupil of the Venerable Bede, under whose direction academies were established. The sons of the more wealthy flocked to his lectures. Alcuin spoke Latin, Greek, and Hebrew, was master of philosophy, theology, history and mathematics. Under his direction the schools of the Empire became celebrated and scholars from all Europe came to learn wisdom at his feet. The impulse thus given to letters by Charlemagne was continued by his successors. The statues of Constantine the Great and Charlemagne grace the vestibule of St. Peter's in Rome.

12. Alfred the Great (A.D. 849 – 899), king of the West Saxons in England. He freed the country of the Danish invaders, codified and promulgated laws, founded monasteries, brought learned men from other lands, gave proof of his own learning by translating several important works into Anglo-Saxon.

13. See Author's *Origines de la Civilisation Moderne* (The Origins of Modern Civilization), 6th edition.

14. The Waldenses derived their name from Peter Waldo, a rich merchant of Lyons, who gathered around him a number of followers and sent them out two by two to preach in the country districts about Lyon (A.D. 1170). Alexander III praised their zeal, but recommended that they should not interfere with the duties of the clergy. They paid no attention to this advice and were excommunicated at the Council of Verona (A.D. 1184). Their rebellion against the Church naturally led the Waldenses into heresy.

15. Manicheism was propagated by Manes, who was born in Persia in 240. He announced himself as a new apostle of Jesus Christ and proclaimed the existence of two eternal principles - a good and an evil principle.

16. Gregory VII was born in Tuscany, Italy, about 1020; died May 25, 1085. During

# NOTES

the reign of Pope Leo IX he showed great executive ability and a burning desire for reform. At the death of Leo IX, asked by the people and clergy of Rome to become Pope, he had Victor II elected instead. During the reign of this Pontiff, he steadily maintained and even increased the ascendancy which his commanding genius had acquired for him during the pontificate of Leo IX. At the death of Victor II, Hildebrand secured the election of Nicholas II. The decree of election of Pope Nicholas by which the power of choosing the Pope is vested in the College of Cardinals was in large measure the achievement of Hildebrand, whose power and influence had become supreme in Rome. At the obsequies of Alexander II, whom Hildebrand's influences had raised to the pontificate, a loud cry from the whole multitude of clergy and people was heard: "Let Hildebrand be Pope!" On the same day Hildebrand was conducted to the Church of San Pietro in Vincoli, and there elected in canonical form by the assembled Cardinals.

17. Countess Mathilda of Tuscany, or of Canossa, 1046 – 1114, was finely educated, deeply religious and from her youth followed with interest the great ecclesiastical questions of the day. Her domains were of the greatest importance in the political and ecclesiastical disputes of the time, as the road from Germany by way of upper Italy to Rome passed through them. On April 22, 1073, Gregory VII became Pope and before long the great battle for the independence of the Church and the reform of ecclesiastical life began. In this contest Mathilda was the fearless, courageous, generous and unswerving ally of Gregory and his successors. It was at Mathilda's mountain stronghold of Canossa that Henry IV appeared before Gregory VII and atoned for his guilt by public penance.

18. The Cistercian Order is named after its first monastery at Citeaux (Cistercium) in France, where the society was founded in 1098 by St. Robert, under the rule of St. Benedict. St. Bernard was the most celebrated member of the order, and is considered as its second founder. In 1134, after thirty-six years of existence, the order counted seventy monasteries. The Cistercians led a contemplative and very ascetic life.

19. St. Dominic, born in Spain in 1170, founded the Order of the Friars Preachers or Dominicans, in 1215. At the first general chapter held at Bologna in 1220, it was determined that the habit of the Friars Preachers, theretofore called Black Friars, should be white and the order should possess no property.

20. For the practice of poverty St. Francis of Assisi, born in Italy in 1182, founded the Friars Minor or Minorites. Its principal object is the realization of a poverty so perfect that it should be manifested in every way and in all things. The order was formally approved by Honorius III in 1223.

21. Gothic Art. The word Gothic designates the style of architecture which flourished in the western part of Europe from the end of the twelfth century to the revival of the classical styles in the sixteenth century. Generally speaking, the Gothic style is at once the most scientific and the most artistic style of architecture. It is the most scientific, because its whole strength is made to reside in a finely organized and frankly confessed framework rather than in walls. This framework, made up of piers, arches and but-

tresses, is freed from every unnecessary encumbrance and it is rendered as light in all its parts as is compatible with strength. It is the most artistic style because the liberal, harmonious and consistent use of the pointed arch, the threefoil, the quatrefoil, the quinquefoil, foliated capitals, deep mouldings, finials, crockets, four-petaled flowers, etc., enable the artist to make our Gothic buildings pictures of perfect beauty. The Gothic monuments of the Middle Ages are at once the admiration and the despair of modern architects.

22. Scholasticism. This term denotes the method or system of teaching and the doctrines of "The Schoolmen" or philosophers and theologians of the Middle Ages, especially from the eleventh to the sixteenth centuries. They reduced into unity and system the teachings of the philosophers and theologians who had gone before them. The greatest among them was St. Thomas Aquinas. He is called the "Angel of the School." Pope Leo XIII, of glorious memory, in his encyclical, *Aeterni Patris Filius*, urged the Christian world to return to the study of philosophy and theology in accordance with St. Thomas.

23. The author here alludes to St. Louis, King of France, who undertook two crusades against the Muslims and died of fever in 1270, in the course of his second crusade, in his camp near Carthage.

24. St. Ferdinand III (1219 – 1252), conquered the greater part of Andalusia, leaving the Muslims only the kingdom of Granada. The cathedral of Burgos occupies the first place among the monuments of his greatness.

25. The Truce of God was a temporary suspension of hostilities. It was brought into existence to curb the war lust of the feudal lords. A Council of Elne in 1207, in a canon concerning the sanctification of Sunday, forebade hostilities from Saturday night until Monday morning. This prohibition was subsequently extended to the days of the week consecrated by the great mysteries of Christianity, namely, Thursday in memory of the Ascension, Friday, the day of the Passion. Still another step included Advent and Lent in the Truce. The penalty for the violation of the Truce was excommunication. The Truce soon spread from France to Germany and Italy. The ecumenical council of 1179 extended the institution to the whole church.

26. The Crescent, or sign of the increasing moon, was the ancient symbol of Byzantium or Constantinople. After the taking of that City by the Turks in 1453, it became the emblem of the Turkish Empire and the sign and symbol of Islam, just as the Cross is the emblem of the Christian religion.

27. The author refers here to Philip the Fair, king of France, sending William of Nogaret to Anagni in order to seize Pope Boniface VIII.

28. Aristotle (384 – 322 B.C.) Greek philosopher, a pupil of Plato, teacher of Alexander the Great, is considered the greatest heathen philosopher. He wrote the first systematic treatise on logic. He wrote also treatises on metaphysics, physics, biology, zoology, psychology, anthropology, ethics, politics, poetry and rhetoric.

29. Virgil (70 – 19 B.C.). Roman poet; his *Aeneid* is the greatest of the Latin epics.

## NOTES

30. By "Pandects" is meant the digest, or abridgement, in fifty books of the decisions, writings and opinions of the old Roman jurists, made in the sixth century by direction of the Emperor Justinian, and forming the leading compilation of the Roman civil law. It is also called "Corpus Juris" – the body of law.

31. Caligula, Roman Emperor (37 – 41), sent cups of poison to his friends, ordered superannuated or sick gladiators, speculators or prisoners to be thrown to the wild beasts in the arena. When his terrible cruelties drove the people away from the amphitheater, he closed the public granaries. One day, to express his displeasure at the applause in the circus, he exclaimed: "Would that Roman people had but one head, that I might cut it off with one stroke." He was shamelessly immoral.

32. Nero, Roman Emperor (54 – 68), procured the assassination of his own mother, sang verses and accompanied himself on the lyre, whilst watching the conflagration of Rome. When he was accused of having caused the fire he blamed it on the Christians. He ordered the first general persecution against them. Deserted by the people, abandoned even by the praetorians he ordered his grave to be dug; and gazing into it he exclaimed: "How great an artist is about to perish!" Finding no one who was willing to kill him, he stabbed himself.

33. Domitian, Roman Emperor (81 – 96), the equal of any of his predecessors in obscenity, exceeded both Nero and Tiberius in cruelty; but, nevertheless, the Romans called him god, the son of Minerva. Pliny informs us that the streets leading to the Capitol were always bloody with the sacrifice of human victims before his statues. The career of this monster was cut short by his wife who induced one of his freedmen to kill him because he intended to proscribe her. Domitian decreed the second general persecution against the Christians.

34. Commodus, Roman Emperor (180 – 192), devoted much of his time to fighting and killing, in the public arena, opponents whose weapons were always blunt and edgeless, or cripples disguised as wild beasts. Such exhibitions regaled the frequenters of the Circus on seven hundred and thirty-five occasions. After a reign of nearly thirteen years the wretch was poisoned by his closest attendants who had learnt he had ordered their death.

35. Caracalla, Roman Emperor (211 – 217), committed excesses which defy description. In Rome alone, more than twenty thousand persons were executed under the pretext that they were partisans of Geta, brother of Caracalla, whom the latter had treacherously killed in his mother's arms. Caracalla was assassinated in his thirtieth year by Macrinus, prefect of the praetorians.

36. Heliogabulus, an oriental adventurer, a priest of the Sun (whence his name Heliogabalus), became Roman Emperor (218 – 222) through the intrigues of his mother. During his four years of rule his barbarity, immorality and extravagance exceeded those of any who had yet wielded the Roman scepter. Among his ridiculous enactments we note his enrolment of his grandmother among the Conscript Fathers. Heliogabalus was killed by the praetorians.

# THE CHURCH AT THE TURNING POINTS OF HISTORY

37. Letter of May 28, 1295 in the Register of Boniface VIII, col. 295.

38. Letters of April 16th and 17th 1296, in the Register of Boniface VIII, col. 59, et seq.

39. This is the name of Boniface VIII previous to his election to the supreme Pontificate.

40. Clerical immunity, as recognized by the Christian States in the Middle Ages, withdrew the clergy from secular jurisdiction, so that not only spiritual lawsuits of clerics, but also temporal lawsuits, whether criminal or civil, fell exclusively within the jurisdiction of ecclesiastical judges.

41. Alexander III, Pope (1159 -81), foremost as a canonist, and ecclesiastical legislator and a valiant defender of the rights of the Church against the encroachments of kings and emperors; he overcame the violence of the Emperor Barbarossa and compelled Henry II of England to ask pardon for the murder of Thomas à Beckett.

42. Innocent III (1161 – 1216), one of the greatest Popes of the Middle Ages, was a learned theologian and one of the greatest jurists of his time and a strenuous defender of the rights of the Church. He steadily strove to put an end to hostilities among Christian princes. He prepared a crusade against the Moors. He undertook the Fourth Crusade. He extended his beneficent influence practically over the whole Christian world.

43. Dante, *Purgatorio*, XX. 86 – 90.

44. E. Boutaric, *La France sous Philippe le Bel*, p. 94

45. At this point it is refreshing to note how Pope Benedict XIV, from the day of his coronation, did not cease to entreat the belligerent nations to make a just and durable peace, how, in particular, on August 1, 1917, in a letter addressed to the leaders of all the belligerent peoples, compelled by a sentiment of his supreme duty as the common father of the faithful, in the name of the Divine Redeemer, the Prince of Peace, he admonished them to reflect on their very grave responsibility before God and before man, begged them to substitute for the material force of arms the moral force of right, to adopt compulsory arbitration of all national questions in order to reach a just and durable peace.

46. Roger Bacon, English philosopher, born 1214; died at Oxford, perhaps June 11, 1294. He must be reckoned among the most eminent scholars of all time. His chief work is the *Opus Maius*, composed at the request of Pope Clement IV. It is a general treatise on the sciences.

47. Albert the Great, scientist, philosopher, and theologian, born about 1206 in Swabia; died at Cologne, November 15, 1280. He is called "the Great," and "Universal Doctor," in recognition of his extraordinary genius and extensive knowledge. He was proficient in every branch of learning cultivated in his day and surpassed all his contemporaries, except perhaps Roger Bacon (1214 – 94), in the knowledge of nature. He

# NOTES

was a priest of the Dominican Order. He was beatified in 1622 and the Bishops of Germany, in 1872, sent to the Holy See a petition for his canonization.

48. Vincent of Beauvais undertook a systematic and comprehensive treatment of all branches of human knowledge in his great work, *Speculum Majus*. This book treats of theology, philosophy, natural sciences, medicine, surgery, jurisprudence, history and literature. The *Speculum Majus* contains 80 books divided into 9,885 chapters, figures which give some idea of the magnitude of the work accomplished by the Dominican priest in the first half of the thirteenth century.

49. Rudolph Agricola (Huysmann), born in Holland about 1443, died at Heidelberg, Germany, 1485. He was renowned for the study of the ancients, the elegance of his Latin style, his knowledge of philosophy, Hebrew and Scripture. He zealously promoted the study of classics in Germany. He was deeply religious.

50. Aleandro Girolamo (1480 – 1542), a humanist. He went to Paris in 1508, gave lectures in Greek, Latin and Hebrew and was made rector of the university. Later he became papal nuncio in Germany to deal with Luther's case. He was created archbishop of Brindisi, Italy, and a cardinal.

51. Jacopo Sadoleto, cardinal, humanist and reformer, born at Modena, Italy, 1477; died at Rome 1547. He was versed in the various branches of Latin and Italian culture. He was secretary to Leo X. In 1517 he was appointed bishop of Carpentras, near Avignon, France. Unlike many of the humanists, he was a man of blameless life and attentive to all his duties as a priest and bishop. As poet, orator, theologian and philosopher, he was in the foremost rank of his time.

52. Marco Girolamo Vida, humanist, born at Cremona, Italy, about 1490; died in 1566. He is the author of a great Christian epic, *Christias*. He also wrote, *De Arte Poetica*, inspired by the ancient Roman writer Quintillion. Vida's style is clear, elegant, harmonious and ordinarily simple.

53. Giovanni Pico della Mirandola, Italian philosopher and scholar, born 1463; died 1494. He devoted himself to the study of philosophy and theology, Greek, Latin, Syriac and Arabic. Towards the end of his life he destroyed his poetical works, gave up profane science and determined to give his time to the defense of Christianity against Jews, Muslims and Astrologers. Savonarola delivered his funeral oration.

54. Alexander Hegius, humanist; born probably in 1433, at Heeck, Westphalia; died 1498. He was ordained a priest when of quite mature age. He spoke and wrote a pure Ciceronian Latin, and was equally versed in Greek. He established a school for the study of these languages in Holland and simplified and improved the method of teaching.

55. St. Thomas More, knight, Lord Chancellor of England, author and martyr, born in London about 1477, executed at Tower Hill, July 6, 1535. He studied at Oxford, mastered the Greek and Latin languages, French, history, mathematics and law; was made a lecturer on law; wrote poetry, both Latin and English; cultivated the acquaintance of learned men, of Erasmus, among others. Besides law and the classics he read the

writings of the ancient Fathers. For some time he considered the question of becoming a priest. He decided to practise law, in which profession he scored immediate success. On July 1, 1535 More was indicted for high treason at Westminster Hall before a special commission of twenty, on the charge of denying Parliament's power to confer ecclesiastical supremacy on Henry VIII. He was found guilty, sentenced to death, and executed five days later. St. Thomas More was formally beatified by Pope Leo XIII, December 26, 1886. Of all his writings the most famous is the *Utopia*.

56. St. John Fisher, cardinal, Bishop of Rochester, and martyr; born at Beverly, Yorkshire, England, 1459; died June 22, 1535. At Cambridge he received successively the degrees of BA in 1487, MA in 1491, DD in 1501, was elected Vice-Chancellor in 1501, Chancellor in 1504, to which post he was re-elected annually for ten years and then appointed for life. Aside from his share in the Lady Margaret's foundations, Fisher gave further proof of his genuine zeal for learning by inducing Erasmus to visit Cambridge. He is the author of twenty-six works in all, several of which have been reprinted several times. He denied the spiritual supremacy of the king; opposed openly the divorce of Henry VIII and Catherine of Aragon and refused to acknowledge the legitimacy of the offspring of Henry VIII and Anne Boleyn. He was sent to the Tower of London on April 26, 1534, sentenced to death and executed. He was formally beatified by Pope Leo XIII in 1886.

57. Juan Luis Vives, Spanish humanist and philosopher, born at Valencia in 1492; died at Bruges, Belgium, May 6, 1540. He first studied at the University of Paris, 1519, was appointed professor at the University of Louvain, where he was associated with Erasmus; in 1523 he became attached to the Corpus Christi College, Oxford, was banished from England for opposing the divorce of Henry VIII. He is the author of numerous works of great merit and popularity, on Christian piety, teaching and education, political economy and philosophy. He also showed himself an organizer of public relief.

58. Cleynaerts, Belgian priest and Orientalist. His thorough knowledge of the Hebrew and Arabic languages, literature and history led him to advocate preaching to the Jews and the Muslims rather than fighting them with the sword. He strove to establish at Louvain, a seminary for training priests for missionary work among Muslims. He spent some months in Africa evangelizing the followers of Mohammed. He died in Granada, Spain.

59. Troubadours, lyrical poets who flourished from the eleventh to the latter part of the thirteenth century, principally in southern France, Catalonia, Aragon, and northern Italy. Their poetry was characterized by an almost exclusive devotion to the subject of chivalric love.

60. *Minnesingers* were German lyric poets and singers of the twelfth and thirteenth centuries, so-called because love was the chief theme of their poems.

61. *Chanson de Roland*, a French epic, put into writing about the year 1080, and by an unknown author, is the most celebrated of the history songs of the Middle Ages. It is the story of the death of Roland at Roncesvalles and Charlemagne's vengeance. It places vividly before the imagination the France of those times, warlike, violent, but

## NOTES

animated with an ardent faith. It has been recently done into English, in the original measure, by Mr. Charles Scott Moncrieff, under the title, *The Song of Roland* - Chapman & Hall, London.

62. *Poem of the Cid* or *Romances of the Cid*, a Spanish poem composed by an unknown author about 1200. The Cid is the principal national hero of Spain, famous for his exploits in the wars with the Moors. The poem is a spirited exhibition of national peculiarities in the chivalrous times of Spain.

63. *Nibelungenlied* or *Song of Nibelungen*, a Middle High German epic, the greatest monument of early German in the first half of the thirteenth century. The Nibelungen, in the German legend, were a race of Northern dwarves, conquered by the mythological hero, Siegfried.

64. *The Roman de Renard* is a vast collection, formed early in the thirteenth century, of stories in verse thrown together without sequence or connection. In all its parts the same hero appears again and again, "Renard" the fox. The action round about Renard is carried on by many other characters, such as the wolf, the lion, the cock, pseudo-animals that mingle with their bearing and instinct as animals, traits and feelings borrowed from humanity. It is a kind of parody of the "history songs." It ridicules the nobles, feudal society and feudal institutions.

65. "The awful mysteries of religion are not susceptible of cheerful ornaments."

66. The Grove of Academus was the resort where Plato, the great Greek philosopher, taught for nearly fifty years until his death in 348 B.C.

67. Louis Adolphe Thiers (1797 – 1877), French journalist, statesman and historian.

68. *Mestier non era partorir Maria,* Dante, *Purgatorio,* III, 39.

69. Epaminondas, Theban general, who defeated the Spartans at Leuctra in 371 B.C., and was victorious and mortally wounded at Mantinea in 362 B.C.

70. *The Imitation of Christ* was at first published anonymously in 1418. Its authorship was until recently in dispute, being attributed to various spiritual writers, St. Bernard, St. Bonaventure, Innocent III, Walter Hilton, Giovanni Gersen and others. The authorship of St. Thomas à Kempis has been completely established in recent years.

71. Inasmuch as an authority like Kurth, and the best Catholic historians generally, have agreed in a very unfavorable judgment of Alexander VI, it is very interesting to note that the Rev. P. De Roo, author of *The History of America Before Columbus,* maintains that the verdict of history regarding Alexander VI should be entirely reversed, that the case of this Pontiff is an astonishing case of complete calumniation by the hostile writers of his time. Fr. De Roo is preparing a *Life of Alexander VI* in which he promises to prove his contention by means of hitherto unstudied documents, especially from the secret archives of the Vatican.

72. Charles V was a reader of Machiavelli. His ungallant remark at the raising of the siege of Metz: "Fortune is a woman, she does not love old men," was inspired by *The*

# THE CHURCH AT THE TURNING POINTS OF HISTORY

*Prince* of Machiavelli, ch. XXV.

73. John Calvin, born at Noyon, France in 1509, and died at Geneva, 1564. In Geneva the clergy, assisted by the elders, governed despotically and in detail the actions of every citizen. In this matter Geneva set an example to the later Puritans, who did all in their power to imitate its discipline.

74. Bramante (1444 – 1514), Italian painter and architect, designed St. Peter's in Rome. His work in Milan is characterized by a pronounced picturesque decorative style, whilst his artistic productions in Rome are, as far as possible, free from all external decorations, and impressive by reason of their proportions, grandeur and power.

75. Michelangelo (Buonarotti), 1475 – 1564, Italian sculptor, painter and architect, one of the greatest artists of all times. At the request of Pope Julius II he painted the world renowned frescoes of the Creation, the Fall, the Preparation for the Coming of the Redeemer, and the Last Judgment in the Sistine Chapel of the Vatican.

76. Raphael (Raffaele Sanzio d'Urbino), 1483 – 1520, Italian painter, the founder of the Roman school of painting of the Renaissance. He was pre-eminent as a draftsman, a colorist, and a master of graceful composition and remarkable for the wide range of his subjects and the great variety of his style. He painted the world renowned "Transfiguration" and "Sistine Madonna."

77. In order to reform existing abuses, Louis XVI, in compliance with the universal request of all classes of the French people, convened the States-General, or the assembly of the three orders of the kingdom, namely, the Clergy, the Nobility, and the Third Estate or Commonality. These had not been in session since 1614.

78. The Third Estate, having as many members as the other two orders of the States-General combined, insisted on voting per head instead of per order, and thus obtained the preponderance in the States-General. The new assembly thus formed with the Third Estate in control was called the Constituent Assembly, because it had for its object the formation of a constitution.

79. Robespierre, born at Arras, May 6, 1759. He was an advocate; was elected to the Third Estate of the States-General in 1789; became the leader of the Extreme Left in the Constituent Assembly, and one of the foremost orators of the Revolution. He was elected deputy to the Convention in 1792; was identified with the "Reign of Terror"; was overthrown in the Convention, July 27, 1794, the 9th Thermidor, year II of the Republican calendar, and guillotined the next day.

80. The Assembly of Notables, a council of prominent persons from the three classes of the State convoked by the kings on extraordinary occasions. The most famous assemblies were those of 1787 and 1788, summoned by Louis XVI. In the assembly of 1787 there were only twenty-seven representatives of the Third Estate out of a total of a hundred and forty-four members.

81. Jacques-Bénigne Bossuet, a celebrated French writer and pulpit orator (1627 – 1704), was appointed preceptor to the Dauphin for whose benefit he wrote, among other

## NOTES

things, the greatest book of the century of Louis XIV, *Discourse on Universal History*. Later he was appointed Bishop of Meaux. He is the author of numerous spiritual, historical polemical works, and, in the words of St. Simon, "died fighting." Ferdinand Brunetière, the eminent French critic, says: "There is nothing, in French, which surpasses a fine page of Bossuet."

82. Frederick II, "The Great" (1740 – 1788), King of Prussia, which country he raised to the rank of a great power. He early became a free-thinker. He praised the literature of France and despised that of Germany. He was an intimate friend of Voltaire.

83. Catherine II (1729 – 1796), Empress of Russia, extended the limits of the Russian Empire by victories over the Turks, secularized the property of the clergy, became famous as a writer, and corresponded with the French Encyclopedists.

84. Jean Jacques Rousseau born at Geneva, June 28, 1712; died near Paris, July 2, 1778. His book, *Contrat Social*, has been styled "the Koran of the Revolutionists."

85. Jean Racine, the most celebrated French tragic poet, born December 21, 1639; died at Paris, April 26, 1699. His masterpiece is *Athalie*, a scriptural tragedy.

86. Minos, ancient King of Crete, and law-giver of that island.

87. Marat, born in Switzerland in 1744, assassinated at Paris in 1793 by Charlotte Corday. He was a leader of the Commune. He had two leading ideas which the Committee of Public Safety subsequently realized – extermination in mass of the enemies of the Revolution – and the appointment of a dictator, whose functions should be limited to proscribing.

88. George-Jacques Danton, born October 28, 1759; guillotined at Paris, April 5, 1794. He was an orator of great power, a leader of the attack on the Tuileries, was implicated in the "September massacres." He overthrew Hébert and his party with the aid of Robespierre and was in turn overthrown by the latter.

89. Feuillants, a political faction of the Revolution which received its name from the Convent of the Feuillants where it held its first meetings.

90. Girondists, an important political party during the French Revolution. Their original leaders came from the department of Gironde, hence their name. They were moderate Republicans, were the ruling party in 1792, were overthrown in the Convention in 1793.

91. Jacobins, members of a society of French revolutionists organized in 1789, and called Jacobins from the Jacobin convent in Paris where they met. The more violent members speedily gained the control of the organization, supported Robespierre and brought on the "Reign of Terror."

92. Cordeliers, a political club which took its name from its meeting place in the Convent of the Cordeliers. Its first political move was to demand the deposition of the king and the establishment of a republic, on June 20, 1791. It was extinguished with the "Reign of Terror" in 1794. Danton was its political chief.

# THE CHURCH AT THE TURNING POINTS OF HISTORY

93. Thermidorians, the more moderate party of the French Revolution, who took part in or sympathized with the overthrow of Robespierre and his adherents on the 9th of Thermidor, year II (July 27, 1794).

94. The Directory, a body of five men who held the executive power in France from November 1, 1795, to the coup d'état of November 9, 1799. The Directory was overthrown by Napoleon, and succeeded by the Consulate.

95. Montagne (Mountain). Name given to the extreme revolutionary party in the legislatures of the first French Revolution, derived from the fact that they occupied the higher part of the hall. Among the chief Montagnards were Robespierre and Danton.

96. This anecdote is told of Cambacérès by Baron, *Mosaïque Belge*, 1837, p. 183.

97. When Clement XIV ascended the throne of Peter, France, Spain and Portugal had suppressed the Society of Jesus *de facto*; the accession of a new Pope was made the occasion for insisting on the abolition of the Order, root and branch, *de facto* and *de jure*, in Europe and all over the world. This persecution was inspired in Latin countries by French irreligious philosophism, by Jansenism, Gallicanism and Erastianism. An ever-recurring and almost solitary grievance against the Society was the Fathers disturbed the peace wherever they were firmly established. The accusation was not unfounded; the Jesuits did, and to the present day do, disturb the peace of the enemies of the Church. In 1772, the Spanish ambassador threatened the Pope with a schism in Spain and probably in other Latin countries, such as had existed in Portugal from 1760 to 1770. This contemptible threat broke the backbone of the opposition of Clement XIV who, the following June, signed the brief of suppression to restore the peace of the Church by removing one of the contending parties from the battlefield. No blame was laid by the Pope on the rules of the Order, or the personal conduct of the members, or the orthodoxy of their teaching.

98. L'abbé Sicard, *Le Clergé de l'ancien régime, les évêques*, tome II, p. 114.

99. "The Great Turk leaves the Christians free to elect and depose their pastors. If the Church of France were in the same condition, we should have the liberty, we do not now possess, of electing, deposing and assembling our pastors." (*Oeuvres de Fénelon*, ed. F. Didot, 1861, tome III, p. 432.)

100. *L'Esprit des Lois* (The Spirit of Laws) written by Montesquieu, fourteen years before the *Contrat Social* of Rousseau. Its political influence was worldwide. But on various points he seriously misunderstood Catholic teaching, and the Sorbonne drew up a list of passages from his writings that seemed to call for censure (August 1752).

101. The Society of Jesus was restored by Pius VII, August 7, 1814, by the bull, *Solicitudo Omnium Ecclesiarum*.

102. How the principles of St. Thomas furnish a remedy for the evils affecting modern society is explained in the great encyclicals of Leo XIII on *The Christian Constitution of States, Human Liberty, The Chief Duties of Christians as Citizens*, and *The Condition of the Working Classes*.

# *More* titles available direct from IHS Press.

*The Outline of Sanity,* by G.K. Chesterton
184pp, 6"x9", ISBN 0-9714894-0-8, Item No. GKC001 **$14.95**

*The Free Press,* by Hilaire Belloc
96pp, 5½"x8½", ISBN 0-9714894-1-6, Item No. HB001 **$8.95**

*Action: A Manual for the Reconstruction of Christendom,* by Jean Ousset
272pp, 6"x9", ISBN 0-9714894-2-4, Item No. JO001 **$16.95**

*An Essay on the Restoration of Property,* by Hilaire Belloc
104pp, 5½"x8½", ISBN 0-9714894-4-0, Item No. HB002 **$8.95**

*Utopia of Usurers,* by G.K. Chesterton
136pp, 5½"x8½", ISBN 0-9714894-3-2, Item No. GKC002 **$11.95**

*Irish Impressions,* by G.K. Chesterton
152pp, 5½"x8½", ISBN 0-9714894-5-9, Item No. GKC003 **$12.95**

*The Church and the Land,* by Fr. Vincent McNabb
192pp, 6"x9", ISBN 0-9714894-6-7, Item No. VM001 **$14.95**

*Capitalism, Protestantism and Catholicism,* by Amintore Fanfani
192pp, 6"x9", ISBN 0-9714894-7-5, Item No. AF001 **$14.95**

*Twelve Types,* by G.K. Chesterton
96pp, 5½"x8½", ISBN 0-9714894-8-3, Item No. GKC004 **$8.95**

*The Gauntlet: A Challenge to the Myth of Progress,* A first anthology of the writings of Arthur J. Penty
96pp, 5½"x8½", ISBN 0-9714894-9-1, Item No. AP001 **$8.95**

*Flee to the Fields,* the papers of the Catholic Land Movement
160pp, 5½"x8½", ISBN 0-9718286-0-1, Item No. FF001 **$12.95**

*An Essay on the Economic Effects of the Reformation,* by George O'Brien
160pp, 5½"x8½", ISBN 0-9718286-2-8, Item No. GO001 **$12.95**

*Charles I,* by Hilaire Belloc
288pp, 6"x9", ISBN 0-9718286-3-6, Item No. HB003 **$16.95**

*Charles II: the Last Rally,* by Hilaire Belloc
224pp, 6"x9", ISBN 0-9718286-4-4, Item No. HB004 **$15.95**

*A Miscellany of Men,* by G.K. Chesterton
184pp, 5½"x8½", ISBN 0-9718286-1-X, Item No. GKC005 **$13.95**

*Distributist Perspectives,* Vol. I, by the chief Distibutists
96pp, 5½"x8½", ISBN 0-9718286-7-9, Item No. DP001 **$8.95**

*Dollfuss: An Austrian Patriot,* by Fr. Johannes Messner
160pp, 5½"x8½", ISBN 0-9718286-6-0, Item No. JM001 **$12.95**

*Economics for Helen,* by Hilaire Belloc
160pp, 5½"x8½", ISBN 1-932528-03-2, Item No. HB006 **$12.95**

*Richelieu,* by Hilaire Belloc
272pp, 6"x9", ISBN 0-9718286-8-7, Item No. HB005 **$16.95**

*The Guild State,* by G.R.S. Taylor
128pp, 5½"x8½", ISBN 1-932528-00-8, Item No. GT001 **$11.95**

*The Party System,* by Hilaire Belloc and Cecil Chesterton
160pp, 5½"x8½", ISBN 1-932528-11-3, Item No. HB007 **$12.95**

*Neo-CONNED!,* by Pat Buchanan, Jude Wanniski, Sam Francis, et al
447pp, 6"x9", ISBN 1-932528-04-0, Item No. NC01 **$19.95** (paperback)

*Neo-CONNED! Again,* by Robert Fisk, Robert Hickson, Donn de Grand Pré, et al
897pp, 6"x9", ISBN 1-932528-05-9, Item No. NC02 **$29.95** (paperback)

**Order direct today:** by phone, fax, mail, e-mail, online.
**s/h:** $3.50 per book; $1.50 ea. add'l. book. Check, m.o., VISA, MC.

*See the other side of this page for contact information.*

# About IHS Press

IHS Press believes that the key to the restoration of Catholic Society is the recovery and the implementation of the wisdom our Fathers in the Faith possessed so fully less than a century ago. At a time when numerous ideologies were competing for supremacy, these men articulated, with precision and vigor, and *without* apology or compromise, the only genuine alternative to the then- (and still-) prevailing currents of thought: value-free and yet bureaucratic "progressivism" on the one hand, and the rehashed, *laissez-faire* free-for-all of "conservatism" on the other. That alternative is the Social Teaching of the Catholic Church.

Catholic Social Teaching offers the solutions to the political, economic, and social problems that plague modern society; problems that stem from the false principles of the Reformation, Renaissance, and Revolution, and which are exacerbated by the industrialization and the secularization of society that has continued for several centuries. Defending, explaining, and applying this Teaching was the business of the great Social Catholics of last century. Unfortunately, much of their work is today both unknown and unavailable.

Thus, IHS Press was founded in September of 2001A.D. as the only publisher dedicated exclusively to the Social Teaching of the Church, helping Catholics of the third millennium pick up where those of last century left off. IHS Press is committed to recovering, and *helping others to rediscover*, the valuable works of the Catholic economists, historians, and social critics. To that end, IHS Press is in the business of issuing critical editions of works on society, politics, and economics by writers, thinkers, and men of action such as Hilaire Belloc, Gilbert Chesterton, Arthur Penty, Fr. Vincent McNabb, Fr. Denis Fahey, Jean Ousset, Amintore Fanfani, George O'Brien, and others, making the wisdom they contain available to the current generation.

It is the aim of IHS Press to issue these vitally important works in high-quality volumes and at reasonable prices, to enable the widest possible audience to acquire, enjoy, and benefit from them. Such an undertaking cannot be maintained without the support of generous benefactors. With that in mind, IHS Press was constituted as a not-for-profit corporation which is exempt from federal tax according to Section 501(c)(3) of the United States Internal Revenue Code. Donations to IHS Press are, therefore, tax deductible, and are especially welcome to support its continued operation, and to help it with the publication of new titles and the more widespread dissemination of those already in print.

For more information, contact us at:

mail: 222 W. 21ˢᵗ St., Suite F-122~Norfolk, VA 23517 USA
toll-free telephone or fax: 877-IHS-PRES (877.447.7737)
e-mail: order@ihspress.com • internet: www.ihspress.com

IHS Press is a tax-exempt 501(c)(3) corporation; EIN: 54-2057581.
Applicable documentation is available upon request.

www.ingramcontent.com/pod-product-compliance
Lightning Source LLC
Chambersburg PA
CBHW060456080526
44584CB00015B/1451